HOW DID I GET SO BUSY?

The 28-Day Plan to Free Your Time,

Reclaim Your Schedule, and Reconnect

with What Matters Most

Valorie Burton

BROADWAY BOOKS
NEW YORK

PUBLISHED BY BROADWAY BOOKS

Published in the United States by Broadway Books, an imprint of
The Doubleday Broadway Publishing Group, a division
of Random House, Inc., New York.
www.broadwaybooks.com

BROADWAY BOOKS and its logo, a letter B bisected on the diagonal,
are trademarks of Random House, Inc.

Many of the names and identifying characteristics of the individuals
depicted in this book have been changed to protect their privacy. Some
of the individuals described are composites of two or more people.

Book design by Diane Hobbing of Snap-Haus Graphics

Library of Congress Cataloging-in-Publication Data

Burton, Valorie, 1973–
    How did I get so busy? : the 28-day plan to free your time, reclaim your
  schedule, and reconnect with what matters most / Valorie Burton.—1st ed.
      p.   cm.
   1. Time management. 2. Self-management (Psychology) 3. Conduct of
life. I. Title.

BF637.T5B87 2007
640'.43—dc22   2007024324

ISBN 978-0-7679-2622-5

PRINTED IN THE UNITED STATES OF AMERICA

10 9 8 7 6 5 4 3 2

To you, the reader.
I trust our paths have crossed for a purpose.

contents

HOW DID I
GET SO BUSY?

How Busy
Are You?

> I think it is important that the question of managing
> time be addressed in a realistic manner. The reality
> is that everyone feels pressed for time and it is not
> going to change as we become more technologically
> advanced and everything we do can be done in an
> instant by allegedly "working smarter, not harder."
> I want to know, how do I find more time without
> cutting my standard of living?
>
> —MONA, 32

Do you find yourself rushing from one activity to the next, from the time you wake up in the morning until you go to sleep at night? Has your to-do list grown from just a list in your day planner to scraps of paper and Post-its scattered all over your office and home? Is your social life disappearing because you don't have time for friends and fun? And do you feel that lately life has become the proverbial rat race—where you are constantly moving forward at an ever-more-frantic pace, yet experiencing very little of the joys and rewards life has to offer?

If you are like most people, you're probably running nearly all the time. I've been there, as have many of my clients over the years. No doubt you'd like for your schedule to be different, or have even found yourself thinking, "I really need to make a change." When "busyness" becomes all-consuming, many of us know deep down that something's got to give—but we're too busy to figure out how or what that change should be!

I believe that your path has crossed mine and that you've picked up this book for a reason: so that you can finally take control of your schedule, create room to breathe, and make time for the people and activities that matter most. The problem with being too busy is that you lose your sense of self. In the race to get it all done, you give up the experience of being fully engaged in anything. The joys of life, such as a meaningful conversation or a healthy, home-cooked meal, become hassles or impediments to getting other things done. The commitments you love, like your work or favorite hobbies, can become burdensome because they only add to your heavy load. Fortunately, change doesn't have to be difficult. It must, however, be intentional.

Close your eyes for a moment and imagine your life filled with what brings you happiness, peace, and success—at a pace that feels good and with a level of activity that gives you energy rather than saps it. Your life can be different—just 28 days from now. It begins with your decision to change. I will help you delve deep . . . so you can notice the fears that ultimately crowd your schedule with things you don't really want or need to do. I will help you get real about what you can actually accomplish in a day. And I will walk with you every step of the way.

Busyness was my way of life for years, and I was afraid to make a change—afraid that not being busy would mean my career would suffer, and hence my income would suffer, too; afraid that if I wasn't busy, then something must be wrong; and afraid to say "no" to people when their requests left me feeling overloaded with another "to-do." It wasn't until my busy lifestyle became a burden that I realized how out of balance my life was. Love and friendships take nurturing. Good health, a body you love, and time for rest and relaxation require intentional actions. All of this takes time, yes, but there is enough time in the day to do what you were created to do. They key is identifying what's essential at this stage of your journey. For the next 28 days, I will guide you step-by-step toward understanding how you've become so busy and taking the actions that will empower you to free your time, reclaim your schedule, and reconnect with what matters most.

To be clear, this book is not about time management. It's not about getting organized. It is about *you*. It is about helping you get clear about what has driven you to overload your schedule and create the kind of lifestyle that allows you enough space to be your best self, experience the best in your relationships, and reach your potential in your work. Of course, whenever we set out to make a change, there is often that little internal voice that begins chiming in with doubts and pessimism. "You don't really think you can take control of your schedule in just 28 days, do you? You want success *and* time to rest, have fun, and spend quality time with your spouse, significant other, family, and friends? Get real!" Refuse to let that voice dissuade you. Getting real is exactly what you are doing. The way you've been living isn't working for you—that's the reality. And now is the time to do something about it.

As life moves faster, we are compelled to do more. As a result, our lives aren't just overloaded, but lived in overdrive. It is an epidemic that, for many of us, is spiraling out of control. There's little time to live in the present because we're always focused on what needs to be done next. So we're here physically, but mentally we're ten minutes or even ten days into the future. Isn't it draining to wake up daily and spend each day hurrying through a flurry of back-to-back activities, then fall into bed exhausted so that you can wake up and do it all over again? It's time to take back your schedule and your life. I've written *How Did I Get So Busy?* to help you do just that.

Most people look for the quick fix, but this book is an invitation to begin what I call a *self-care lifestyle.* That is, one in which your everyday life reflects who you truly are, engages you in the relationships and activities that you truly love, and gives you the opportunity to relax, reflect, and replenish your energy. If you prefer the simple fixes, you'll find some terrific high-impact ideas here that will help you lighten your load. But I hope that instead, you will accept my invitation and make lasting adjustments to adapt to a new way of living.

Many of the shifts I will encourage you to make are ones you've probably been longing to make for some time. Your journey through these pages will be a practical, but also a soul-nourishing, one. It is not enough to talk about what you need to do differently; you must also take a deeper look at who you really are and the motivating forces and fears that drive you. Without assessing our internal battles, it is impossible to make a permanent change. My goal is not only to help you become less busy, but also more fruitful, well rounded, and productive. My hope is that when you have finished this 28-day program, you will be inspired to adopt these changes as an ongoing way of life.

Before you begin taking steps to tame your overloaded lifestyle, let's find out just how busy you actually are.

How Busy Are You?

Go through the following list and check all of the statements below that are true for you; then give yourself one point for each statement checked:

- ☑ I feel as though I am constantly trying to catch up at work.
- ☑ I feel as though I am constantly trying to catch up with personal responsibilities.

- ☑ My life feels out of balance.
- ☐ My breathing right now is shallow.
- ☑ I am regularly late to appointments and scheduled activities.
- ☐ There's rarely a break in my schedule.
- ☐ My shoulders are not relaxed right now.
- ☐ I eat lunch at my desk at least once per week.
- ☐ I sometimes work straight through lunch.
- ☑ I have not had a vacation longer than seven days in the last year.
- ☐ A seven-day vacation? I've never even had one of those.
- ☑ I have not gotten together with friends for fun and conversation in over a month.
- ☑ Keeping up with household chores is a struggle because of time constraints.
- ☑ I am dissatisfied with the amount of quality time I am able to spend with my spouse or significant other.
- ☑ I am dissatisfied with the amount of quality time I am able to spend with my child.
- ☑ I don't take time to exercise.
- ☐ I resent the things I do for family or friends because I have little or no time for myself.
- ☐ The fuel light in my car has come on at some point in the last two months because I have not had time to fill it up.
- ☑ My mail is piled up because I haven't had time to open or sort it.
- ☑ I have missed paying a bill on time in the last three months because I was too busy to notice the due date had passed.
- ☑ I sometimes run out of socks, jeans, or other clothing items because I haven't had time to do the laundry.
- ☑ I don't have time to write thank-you notes.

☑ My to-do list rarely gets completely checked off for the day.

☑ I work late more than once per week.

☐ At least once per week, I skip meals because I am too busy.

16

Reality Check: How Busy Are You?

1 – 5 Points • Busy
Your schedule is challenging at times, but you are managing to get by. A few small changes will make a big difference toward helping you to take complete control of your time.

6 – 10 Points • Too Busy
Either life is becoming increasingly too busy for you, or you've been managing to get by but are starting to lose control. By taking action over these next 28 days, you can finally take charge of your schedule and decrease the stress that has been building.

11 – 16 Points • Too Busy and Frustrated
Life has been hectic for a while and if you don't slow down soon and become more intentional about where and how you focus your time, you will soon burn out. It is essential that you begin to take steps *now* so you can get your life back.

17 – 25 Points • Out of Control
I understand. I've been there. And it's possible for you to transform how you live so that your schedule is aligned with what's most important to you. It may require some big changes, but remember that change is about making choices. I will invite you to make those choices as we journey through these pages together.

Sometimes it takes a reality check like this one to help you see how busy you are. If busyness has overtaken you, there are signs that will tell you so—and I am glad to know you are listening.

Before writing this book, I surveyed more than 300 adults about the effects of busyness on their lives. Some are married (60 percent) while others are single (40 percent). Many are parents (61 percent). The respondents have a variety of occupations—teacher, lawyer, administrative assistant, professional athlete, doctor, social worker, bus driver, web designer, consultant, corporate manager, stay-at-home mom, retiree, and sales associate, to name a few. Of these, 92 percent are between 25 and 54 years old, and 94 percent have at least some college education; 36 percent hold bachelor's degrees and 27 percent hold graduate degrees. You'll see their comments on the busyness of their lives throughout the pages of this book at the start of each chapter. I believe you'll see some of your own story reflected in their stories. Take a look at some of their eye-opening responses:

- *More than 58 percent have not had a seven-day vacation in the last year.*
- *15 percent have never had a vacation lasting at least seven days.*
- *30 percent called in to the office to check voice mail on their last vacation.*
- *Of the parents surveyed, 70 percent feel they do not spend enough time with their children.*
- *Of those married or in a romantic relationship, 80 percent are not satisfied with the consistency and quality of time spent with their spouse or significant other.*
- *54 percent get together with friends less than once a month.*
- *55 percent have not had a friend over to their home in over two months.*

- *39 percent feel that the most stressful aspect of their schedule is work demands.*

- *38 percent say that the most stressful aspect of their schedule is keeping up with household chores.*

- *80 percent say their schedule is somewhat or entirely overcommitted.*

- *72 percent say that most of the time they feel they are trying to catch up with work and personal responsibilities.*

- *76 percent say they feel busier now than they did five years ago.*

The majority of those I surveyed and interviewed are simply not satisfied with the pace of their lives. How about you? Can you relate to some of the above statistics? It seems that many people find themselves racing through life, attempting to check off a series of never-ending to-do lists. In the process, too many neglect to carve out time for themselves and feel guilty about the lack of time they have for the important people in their lives. The speed at which we live and the expectations about how much we can each personally accomplish in a day have increased dramatically in recent years. No doubt you too have felt the pressure of these expectations.

The root of the busyness epidemic lies partly in the fact that many of us—whether we admit it or not—view our busyness as a badge of honor. "How are you doing?" we are asked, and we instinctively reply, "Oh, I'm *so* busy." If we are busy, we feel that we are accomplishing things, we are making an impact, we are living life to the hilt. But the truth is that busyness itself does not guarantee results. In fact, existing in perpetual overdrive often makes it harder to do anything well at all.

Myth vs. Reality

Let's take a look at some of the common myths about busyness—and where our whirlwind of activity falls short.

BUSY VS. FRUITFUL (OR PRODUCTIVE)

Let's clarify the difference between being busy and being productive. The words are often used interchangeably. But they do not have the same meaning. Being productive means effectively accomplishing that which matters most. A productive salesperson, for example, would be the one who generates significant revenue in an abbreviated period of time. A busy salesperson is active, but may or may not be producing the right results.

SUCCESSFUL VS. FULFILLED

Another distinction that is important to make is the one between being successful and being fulfilled. By society's standards, a person is successful when they reap financial gain, status, prominence, or popularity. Being fulfilled is a joyful inner knowing that you are living, working, and loving in a way that satisfies you emotionally and spiritually as well.

OVERFLOWING WITH OPPORTUNITY VS. OVERRUN WITH ACTIVITY

Overflowing with opportunity is about having myriad chances to do what you love and engaging in activities that are an expression of who and what is really important to you. Overrun with activity is about having too much to do, including stuff that you don't want to do, doesn't fulfill your purpose, takes you farther away from who you truly are, or doesn't empower you to serve or contribute in a way that is meaningful to you.

When you are overrun with activity, it usually means you are ready to overhaul some major areas of your life. You are ready for a life makeover because the life you are living is not a full expression of your values and who you are.

Time for a "Busyness" Diet

The news reports say that we are now a nation of overweight, undernourished people. According to the CDC's National Center for Health Statistics, 66 percent of adults over the age of twenty are overweight—32 percent are obese. Of course, those reports are referring to our eating habits. But as a life coach, I've noticed that eating isn't the only thing plaguing us in excess. It's an excess of obligations and commitments—and when it comes to everyday activities, we pile it on. Our schedules are bulging at the seams. The same phenomenon that has resulted in Americans being more overweight than ever has also resulted in our schedules being more demanding than ever. Over time, as portion sizes in restaurants have increased, so have our expectations of what we can reasonably accomplish in a day. Consider the similarities.

Problem: Overweight Body	Problem: Overloaded Schedule
WARNING SIGNS	**WARNING SIGNS**
Too much food	Too much activity
Too much fattening food	Too much work
Eating late at night	Working late at night
Not enough fruits and vegetables	Not enough rest and relaxation
Too much sugar	Too many options vying for your time
Little or no exercise	Little or no exercise
Couch potato	Automatic pilot—keeps doing what s/he's always done, even if it no longer serves a purpose
Won't say "no" to junk food	Won't say "no" to anyone's requests
BOTTOM LINE	**BOTTOM LINE**
Refusing to change your lifestyle can lead to serious health and personal problems.	Refusing to change your lifestyle can lead to serious health and personal problems.

This book is a kind of busyness "diet"—a lifestyle shift away from living a life that is overloaded and overdriven to living in a way that is managed intentionally. It is what I call a self-care lifestyle. That is, an everyday life in which you live your purpose, have time for the people you love, activities you enjoy, a job that inspires, and most especially time *for you*. It nurtures and supports a balance of personal and professional success. Some will tell you that it is not possible to have both—you must have one or the other. Many will insist that you must be daydreaming if you think you can be ambitious and successful and relaxed all at the same time—don't believe them! I'm not asking you to give up your goals, but to make sure your goals serve a greater purpose, in the right timing and with healthy motives—and that you don't allow what isn't really important to get in the way. Even in the midst of being busy, you can also be at peace about your schedule, and full of energy, passion, and joy.

Throughout the book, we will delve into what I call the Ten Commandments of Self-Care. If you learn to keep them sacred, your life of busyness and overwork will become one of self-care, less stress, and, ultimately, more productivity.

THE TEN COMMANDMENTS OF SELF-CARE

1. Use all of your vacation time every year.
2. Commit your time off solely to nonwork-related activities.
3. Take your rest seriously.
4. Have fun at least once a week.
5. Eat regularly, preferably sitting down.
6. Exercise regularly, preferably standing up.
7. Be fruitful and productive, not busy.
8. Use technology to gain time, not consume it.
9. Connect heart-to-heart with the people who matter.
10. Be led by the Spirit.

What Is Self-Care?

When I began to study life coaching, I embraced the concept and importance of self-care right away. I was ready to focus on nourishing my spirit and doing things that were not about doing more, but were about just "being." It finally dawned on me that if I didn't take extremely good care of me, it would be nearly impossible to care for the people and things that matter most in my life. For our purposes in this book, self-care *is the act of maintaining, nourishing, and protecting your mind, body, and spirit for the purpose of maximizing your effectiveness, happiness, and productiv-*

ity in life. Self-care is not selfish. It is a smart way to live—not overtaxing yourself, doing things that make you feel good about yourself, and continually replenishing your energy to do the work you are meant to be doing. Whether that work is professional, voluntary, or in your own home, self-care empowers you to consistently do it with excellence.

In my first book, *Rich Minds, Rich Rewards*, I made up a word—pamperize. It means prioritize your pampering! Self-care and pampering are often used interchangeably, but pampering is just one aspect of self-care. Self-care also empowers you to nurture and strengthen your relationships, improve your performance at work, dramatically decrease your stress, effectively manage your time, and live the kind of life you have dreamed of. I am not talking about material dreams—although they can be manifested through a consistent self-care regimen—but a fulfilled, joyful life that overwhelms you with gratitude.

Most of us have much to accomplish on a day-to-day basis. I am not here to make you feel guilty about that—or to tell you to quit your job (although that might be the right answer for you) or take a year off to fulfill a dream (another possibility). The reality of an active life is that some aspects are not going to change anytime soon—but that doesn't mean there isn't a better way for you to manage them. The problem is not so much about what you do, but how you go about doing it, the pace at which you do it—and, most important, the truly important things that get left out in the process.

This four-week journey will help you have more of what matters to you—and less of what holds little significance. On this journey I'll share insightful and practical strategies as well as personal stories gleaned from my work coaching professionals and business owners toward more fulfilling, less stressful lives.

The plan in these pages is easy to follow, and over the next four weeks I will coach and support you as you begin making this important lifestyle change. Each day of your 28-day journey, I will challenge you to incorporate these ingredients that nourish your mind, body, and spirit while sifting out those that are currently draining your energy and drowning out those that nurture you. At the end of each "day" or chapter, you will find three specific tools to keep you moving forward on your path:

MY CHALLENGE TO YOU TODAY

This will be a step to take or a decision that I will ask you to make. These challenges are simple, bite-size steps so that you will not be overwhelmed. I know you have plenty to do already, so the challenges are designed to stretch you, but without becoming another to-do on your list. I know it can be tempting when you are reading a book such as this one to skip ahead and not actually do the exercises. But I encourage you to avoid breezing through each chapter. Do the work and I promise it will transform your life! Everything I have written here comes from my personal experience as well as the experiences of countless clients and people just like you, who were tired of being tired and ready for powerful change.

FIVE-MINUTE JOURNAL

Your "five-minute journal" is a tool I recommend you use while reading the book. Each day I will provide you with questions to ponder, and ask you to explore your answers on paper. This self-discovery process will help you uncover crucial answers to important questions in your life. It will help you decide the next steps to take or better understand what the obstacles might be to moving forward and how you can overcome them. If you've never journaled before or feel at all uneasy with the idea, just remember there is no wrong way to do it. Just begin writing the first thing that comes to mind as you answer the questions and let it flow from there. Don't worry about making mistakes; it's the ideas that count rather than the grammar! You will be surprised by the thoughts and feelings that come to the surface and likely amazed at the shifts that can come simply from asking yourself the right questions, then answering them openly and honestly.

ONE-MINUTE MEDITATION

This 28-day journey is about personal growth in the context of spiritual growth, and prayer or meditation can help ground you in a way that nothing else can. It calms you, centers you, and helps you reflect on your life without outside pressure. It is about tuning out what everyone else thinks and tuning in to the divine messages that are available to you when you are quiet enough to listen. You were created for a purpose, and there is enough time in every day for you to accomplish the things that were meant for you to accomplish without becoming overwhelmed or burned out. If there's too much to handle, asking for wisdom about what to change can be an enormous comfort and help. Each day I will give you a statement or a thought to meditate on that will help you conquer the challenge you've been given for that day. The meditation will be a positive affirmation or truth to internalize. To meditate, simply find a quiet spot that feels peaceful. Read the meditation thought for that day, then close your eyes, breathe deeply, and relax. Then focus on the thought.

Since your time is such a precious commodity, you need to meditate for only one minute, though you can certainly meditate longer if you want to. Again, this book is not about giving you more to-do's! It is about helping you discover the life that you were meant to live. Your spiritual well-being is an element of your life that can give you the strength and clarity to take control of the external temptation to do more by focusing inward to create a schedule that fully reflects your heart's desires.

I'm looking forward to supporting and coaching you on your journey over the next 28 days. At the back of the book, you'll find additional space to jot down any extra thoughts and ideas that come to mind. Are you ready to get started? Let's begin!

DAY 1

There Is a Better Way

> By the time I get home, cook dinner, check home-
> work, and do a load of clothes, it's time to get ready
> for the next day. There's no time for anything else.
> If there's a better way, please tell me what it is!
>
> —Suzanne, 37

Since you are reading this book, you likely recognize that your
current lifestyle of busyness and overwork is taking its toll.
You're ready for a break, but unsure of when you can actually
have one. Your schedule may sometimes feel like a cycle that
never stops repeating itself—Monday, Tuesday, Wednesday,
Thursday, Friday, Saturday, Sunday, Monday, Tuesday, Wednesday,
Thursday, Friday . . . Or perhaps, like I once was, you are in a bit
of denial. You don't think there is a real problem. As soon as you
get through this next crunch period, you insist, all will be well.
But when the "crunch period" ends, for some reason, you are
still as busy as ever. All is not well! You are exhausted and it's
time for a change. For years, when people would mention how
busy they thought I was, I would insist that it wasn't that bad. I
had time for myself. They just didn't understand, I reasoned. But
the truth is that I was defensive. And whenever you are defen-

sive about the casual comments people make, there is probably an underlying issue that needs to be addressed.

Let's start by defining what I mean by busy. Being busy is different from hurrying, being productive, hardworking, or rushed—although a busy person may be all of those things. *Webster's Dictionary* describes the word "busy" as follows:

Dictionary Definition	Reality
1. Actively or fully engaged or occupied; "busy with her work"; "a busy man"; "too busy to eat lunch"; "the line is busy."	*As in, you are too occupied to have space for anything else in your life.*
2. Overcrowded or cluttered with detail; "a busy painting"; "a fussy design."	*As in, a life that is too cluttered, crowded, and complicated for you to have clarity and calm.*
3. Intrusive in a meddling or offensive manner; "an interfering old woman"; "bustling about self-importantly making an officious nuisance of himself"; "busy about other people's business."	*As in, fighting unnecessary battles, concerning oneself with things that are not central to your purpose, and allowing others to drain your energy.*
4. Crowded with or characterized by much activity; "a very busy week"; "a busy life"; "a busy street"; "a busy seaport."	*As in, simply having a great deal on your plate.*

5. (Of facilities such as telephones or lavatories) Unavailable for use by anyone else or indicating unavailability; "her line is busy"; "the lavatory is in use"; "kept getting a busy signal."

As in, unavailable to the people who matter most or the opportunities you should take advantage of.

So, in many ways, being busy is characterized by being unavailable for anything else, being fully occupied so that there is no room for anything other than that in which you are already engaged. A life that is too busy is overcrowded and overloaded. In an effort to keep up, we often get through our days in overdrive.

"But that's just the way my life is," you protest, "and I don't see how I can live it any differently. All my friends and coworkers are the same way. How can I really be too busy if it's normal?" Yes, it's normal, but that doesn't mean we shouldn't change it! If you're not sure if you are really too busy, just check for some of the telltale signs. How many of these describe you?

- *Your breathing is shallow.*
- *You never seem to be able to get anywhere on time.*
- *You forget things easily.*
- *You use your vacations, weekends, or holidays to "catch up."*
- *Friends or family members complain that you don't have time for them.*
- *You no longer have the energy to do the things you love to do because they just feel like more items on your to-do list.*
- *You feel scattered or unable to concentrate.*
- *You regularly make mistakes, lose things, and waste money because you are in a hurry.*

Sometimes it can feel as though you are stuck in a rut of over-activity. But you are not stuck. Your life can look very different in just a few short weeks. It's all about the choices you make and the steps you are willing to take forward day by day. It is a joy for me to get to walk alongside you on these pages as you make your shift. Like you, I've had my struggles with overload and overdrive. And I know firsthand that it is possible to be productive without living a cluttered, crowded life. In fact, it's not just possible. I believe it will happen for you.

My Story

Just as I began to write this book about busyness, my already full life became suddenly fuller. My husband and I found a house in a seaside community that we love—so we bought it, sold our house, and moved—all in less than forty days. We had not been planning to move; the circumstances just unfolded and we followed the desires of our hearts. Then two days before the move, a routine physical led to a life-threatening discovery in my family: Doctors informed my father that he had a previously undetected and rare birth defect that, by all accounts, should have taken his life as a child. Miraculously, he was still alive, but he would need corrective open-heart surgery right away to fix it. He stayed with us in the new house during his recovery. Meanwhile, speaking and coaching requests were suddenly more abundant than ever, and I found myself preparing for a speaking schedule that would take me to twelve cities in seven weeks. My biggest concern was for my father—a mix of gratitude and fear. Although my father and all of us around him felt grateful to have discovered this potentially fatal problem so that it could be corrected, and confident that he would make it through, I was still nervous about the prospect of my father going through such a serious surgery. Combined with the move and upcoming schedule, it was a whirlwind of activity. Coincidentally, I had scheduled that entire month to be off— something I'd planned for nearly a year. Although I didn't spend the month with the free time I'd hoped for, the clear schedule gave me the margin I needed to handle a special move to a place we love and the time I needed to be there for my father. It felt so good to have the time to focus on the people and things that really mattered during that time.

I wish I could say that my struggle with busyness was only due to outside pressure, but truth be told, it seems I was wired that way from the time I was a child. As long as I could remember, it seemed my life had been overloaded and in overdrive. I was the kid who took many more classes than she needed to graduate from high school, participated in a sport every season, and juggled student council and at least three other extracurricular activities simultaneously. My parents never pushed me to do it; I was driven on my own, maybe to a fault. Going home right after school was a foreign concept to me. I typically made it home after six or seven every evening and spent many weekends cheering at games, competing in track meets, gymnastics meets, and pageants—and pursuing modeling when I could squeeze it in.

Not surprisingly, I grew up to continue my overload habit into adulthood. By twenty-one, I had finished graduate school. Two years later I quit my job and began working for myself full-time. I replaced a heavy class load and traded student council for professional associations, business meetings, and fund-raising events. I accomplished a lot, but at a great price. I was so focused on the destinations along my path that I usually didn't enjoy the journey much. The focus always seemed to be on the next frontier. The combination of overload and overdrive was overwhelming. And honestly, even though I often looked like I was doing a lot, much of my time was wasted on busywork. There is a difference between being busy and being fruitful or productive. Although I was productive, I was also unnecessarily busy. I procrastinated to the very last minute on many projects, yet managed to get them done well under pressure.

Every few years I seemed to hit a wall. I felt burned out, frustrated—even angry at times. But what was I angry about? No one forced me to pile on the activities and responsibilities. Each time, I created my circumstances and then rebelled against them. I stacked up achievements, but was not satisfied. I had friends, but craved a deeper connection. I was working hard, but yearned to make more money for my efforts. I had a successful business, but little time for success in love. I was oblivious to the idea that life does not have to be lived in a hurry because there was simply always too much to do.

At that time, I didn't know any other way to live than to be busy and on-the-go at all times. I wanted to slow down, but I was afraid I would miss out on something. What, exactly, I didn't know. But as I began peeling back the layers, I discovered that my habitual busyness was a result of several unrelated but intertwined issues. I had never known anything else. I valued achievement more highly than joy, which led to speeding toward the finish line of every project, goal, or task without regard for the gift of the journey. I had bought into the belief that taking on more work, projects, or activities validated my worth, abilities, and potential. Certainly there is nothing wrong with being industrious, but beware when busyness becomes a self-esteem substitute. When I was finally able to lay it all out and confront what had motivated me all these years, I was able to learn several important lessons:

- Faith, family, and friends form the foundation of fulfillment, not achievements, activity, and the approval of others.

- An unclear vision of where you are headed leads to a scattered array of unconnected activities.

- You can always find more to do. It is more challenging to learn to just be.

- Procrastination gives you the illusion that you are busier than you really are.

- Procrastination is a bad habit, and like any other habit, you can break it.

- Perfectionism is not about excellence. It is about fear.

- When you have unresolved issues in one area of life, you are prone to overcompensate in areas in which you feel you have more control.

- Achievement can become an addiction that keeps you frighteningly tethered to the rat race.

- Just because there's more to do doesn't mean it has to be done today.

- Enjoying your journey must be a top priority.

It has taken a great many intentional choices to make a shift—and the journey continues. Like any lifestyle change, it was important for me not to treat just the surface symptoms, but to delve deeper and evaluate my whole life, my approach, and discover where my behaviors stemmed from. Once I came to terms with the lessons above, I was able to adjust my approach to living and working—and to use my experience in my one-on-one work with clients individually and in groups. I simply became tired of being out of balance. I work hard now, but I don't work all the time. It took me a while to notice that my life was all about getting things done—and to decide that I wanted my life to be more than that. It's been a long road to get to the point of being productive, yet well rested—and focused on the things that truly matter most in life.

Let's consider again the first lesson I listed above: Faith, family, and friends form the foundation of fulfillment. Everyone needs a strong foundation on which to live. You are out there in the world accomplishing your unique assignments in life, and you need an anchor to keep you steady. No matter what happens, you need to have sources of unconditional love, joy, and support, a place where it doesn't matter if you succeed or fail. It doesn't matter if you get everything done or do it perfectly. This foundation can hold you up when you are exhausted or weak, energize you when you pursue your dreams, and fire you up to live with purpose. This foundation is comprised of three components: 1) your faith, which is your spiritual life or relationship with God; 2) your family, which can include parents, spouse, children, siblings, and other relatives as well as other loved ones such as a significant other, very close friends, and so forth; and 3) other friends. This foundation is the base of the lifestyle you want to create. That lifestyle can be illustrated as a pyramid similar to a food pyramid. All of the various elements work together to bring health and harmony, and throughout the next 28 days, we'll look closely at each of the five levels and explore how you can enhance each one. Notice that *work* is not the foundation—in fact, it's level #3!

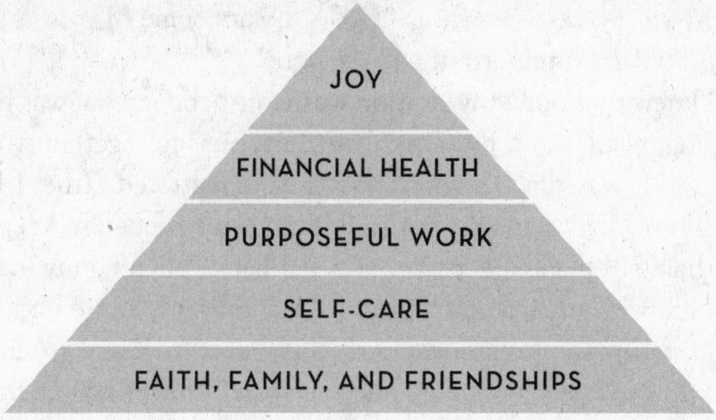
JOY
FINANCIAL HEALTH
PURPOSEFUL WORK
SELF-CARE
FAITH, FAMILY, AND FRIENDSHIPS

Is This a Turning Point for You?

My turning point came when I got married. My husband became a mirror for me and my overloaded, overdriven habits. It is often more difficult for single people, especially those without children, to notice when their lives are out of balance. When the only person you are accountable to is yourself, you can wear yourself into the ground and no one sees you eating cereal for dinner, staying up into the wee hours of the night, or coming in the door at eight or later every evening.

Before we were married, my husband came to visit me (we lived in different states) for New Year's. I am embarrassed to say, I was working. Quite honestly, I didn't think it was a big deal. But he did. "Why did you ask me to come here if you were going to work the whole time?" he asked. In my mind, I was only working a little. Of course, that's because I was not used to being accountable to anyone. Working a little for me regularly turned into working all day. When he said it, I felt a sudden burst of guilt. Deep down I knew I was out of balance, and now here was someone I truly loved and hoped to have a future with essentially pointing out that my habits were affecting him. In so many words, he was saying, "Hello? I want some of your attention, too! How important am I to you?"

I knew that our conversation wasn't just about what was happening on that day, but also about how our life together would unfold. It was time to adjust what really mattered. True, I had always worked that way, but it didn't mean I needed to keep up my habits. I made a decision to begin better aligning my everyday life with my true priorities. I knew that if I wanted a long-term, meaningful relationship, I would need to make space for one. I would need to make some shifts, and little by little, I made them. Interestingly, even though I don't sit at my desk as much as I used to, I am more productive today than I was then—and certainly much less stressed out.

Is today, Day 1, your turning point? Perhaps you are reading this book because this is the right timing for real change. You can learn to put boundaries on your time that increase your productivity and fulfillment level. You can learn to create space in your life despite the number of items on your to-do list. It all begins with your belief that things can be different no matter how difficult they feel right now. There is a better way. And you are about to discover it. The first step on this first day is opening your mind to a new and better way of living. It starts by assessing your situation. We'll do that next.

MY CHALLENGE TO YOU TODAY

Today, declare that change is possible and that you are willing to do what it takes to create change over these 28 days. Open your mind to the possibility of change. Start today by jotting down the areas where you are feeling overwhelmed, overloaded, and/or overdriven. Then imagine for a moment what it will feel like to have control over these areas of your life. Conceiving change is the first step to birthing change.

Five-Minute Journal

In your journal, answer the following questions as openly and honestly as you can (remember, this is for your eyes only): What has led to your current state of busyness? At the end of this 28-day journey, what do you want to be different in your life?

One-Minute Meditation

Something better is possible and will unfold over the next 28 days.

DAY 2

Assess Your
Situation

I have been living in overdrive for some time now and could never understand why I was so anxious and overwhelmed all the time. I am starting to see that my life needs assessing. That alone is an improvement—an acknowledgment that there is a problem to solve.

—JACKIE, 36

On a Monday morning a while ago, I was attempting to slip back into a normal routine after a weekend trip in which I spoke in two cities—fifteen hundred miles apart—in the same day. On a Friday night and Saturday morning, I spoke in Atlanta. Following a book-signing, I headed to the airport to catch a flight to New York City in the afternoon. Amazingly, I had a couple of hours to spare in my hotel room before heading to the venue to speak at eight that evening. The next day at noon I took the train home from New York to Maryland. By 5:00 P.M. on Sunday, I was unpacking and unwinding.

With several projects in process, I had to hit the ground running on Monday morning. The trip had been a success, but there was no time to reflect on it. As I headed to the grocery store that morning, I kept calling my voice mail to leave myself messages as one to-do after another flooded my mind. I was driving and didn't have a notepad. Not that driving and writing would have been a smart option—I'll admit that I have attempted it, although I usually can't make out my writing very well when I go back to read it! The words are choppy and tend to slide downward on the page, getting smaller and less descript as they get closer to the edge—a sure sign you are trying to do too many things at once.

The grocery store is only two miles from home, but before I even reached the parking lot, I was on my fourth "message to self." That's when I got the sign. The conversation went something like this as my voice mail picked up for a fourth time in five minutes:

"This is Valorie Burton. I cannot answer your call right now, but . . ."

I pressed 1 to interrupt the greeting and leave myself a message.

Beep. The system was recording. I said nothing. My mind was absolutely blank. I had no idea why I'd called my voice mail. By now I had pulled into a parking space. I was just sitting there, hands on the steering wheel, earpiece firmly in place, voice mail system dutifully recording my next words.

"Shoot!" I said out loud.

Pause.

"Shoot! What was I about to say?" I demanded, as though I would get a response.

Pause.

"*Why did I call?* Dog-gone it, I can't remember."

Pause.

"Shoot!"

Click.

So it's come to this, I thought. I can't even remember a

thought long enough to call my own voice mail and leave the thought there so that I can remember it later! The pace of my life and the demands of my career and schedule were simply overwhelming—and this was a sign that I needed to do something about it.

Assessing Your Situation

When I initially stepped back and looked at my situation, it seemed hopeless. What's the use of knowing there is a problem if you cannot see how you will change it? That can be downright depressing. So it is tempting to just keep pushing ahead, convincing yourself that this is the way you must live if you want to make money, have friends, or be a good spouse, parent, caretaker, and so forth. The key is to acknowledge the reality of your circumstances without the pressure of having to have an immediate answer for what you will do about it. Acknowledgment is an important part of the assessment process. Assessment includes three easy steps:

1. Accept that there is a problem to be resolved. (Acknowledgment)
2. Write down every responsibility and commitment that you are currently engaged in or will soon be engaged in. (Inventory)
3. Ask yourself, "What do I want my ideal life to look like instead?" (Model)

We will refer to this as the AIM Assessment. AIM stands for—you guessed it: Acknowledgement—Inventory—Model.

Like millions of people, you may not have previously thought of your lifestyle as a serious issue to be resolved. In fact, it's quite possible that many people in your work and personal life lead lives that are just as overloaded and overdriven as your own. What you see around you justifies and even encourages you to keep adding more to your plate. The expectations of you have likely increased over the last five or ten years. Perhaps your job is more demanding, you're married now or you have children or other loved ones to take care of. Maybe you've moved to a new city and have less support from friends and family than you once did. Chances are that you have added more to your load, but you haven't made adjustments that free up more time or space to accommodate these changes. Now it's catching up to you. The first step is to acknowledge that you are too busy and that you can make choices that empower you to do something about it.

Acknowledgment—full acknowledgment—is a critical step on this journey. It can be easy to acknowledge your busyness in one area of your life while remaining in denial about another area. Without acknowledging all areas, it is difficult to truly remedy the problem. For example, when my client Stephanie first came to me, she was frustrated by the number of hours she was putting in at the office. She was driven to see her successful business continue to grow and considering options for delegating some of her responsibilities to a high-level executive. It took some time, but she did it. Yet within a couple of months, she was again feeling the pressure of an overloaded work life. Even though she had delegated responsibility, she had created new projects for herself in order to achieve her larger financial goals.

"What led you to these new goals?" I asked curiously.

"I've been thinking," she explained, "that I need to prepare for retirement and I'm afraid that I'm not going to have enough. I need to make more money so I can save more."

Notice the language that she used, "I'm *afraid* that I'm not going to have enough." Busyness and stress are often rooted in fear—and the fear is often irrational. We'll talk more about this in a few days. But knowing that Stephanie had already built a nice retirement nest egg, I asked, "Why do you need more than you already have? You've mentioned how much it is and that it should be sufficient to serve your needs in retirement, right?" Stephanie went on to explain her fear that her family's high-consumption lifestyle could not be supported on her and her husband's current retirement plans. While her husband earns a respectable living, her income had surpassed his in recent years and their spending kept pace with the earning. Rather than addressing and fixing the hectic pace of her personal expenditures, however, she focused on increasing her pace at work to keep up. In this case, she discovered, the resulting stress was not worth it.

As you acknowledge the ways in which busyness has invaded your life, consider the five key areas:

- *Work*
- *Relationships*
- *Finances*
- *Health and Physical Environments*
- *Spiritual Life*

At this point, you do not need to do anything about it. Only acknowledge that there is a challenge or problem that you want to address.

Now it's time to get specific. What exactly are the activities that are making demands on your time? It may help to take out your PDA or calendar to do an assessment of everything you do on a daily, weekly, monthly, and annual basis. It is easy to leave out the important activities that may occur only annually or biannually—such as a family reunion or vacation—but if you do not account for those as you plan your time, then you will find yourself scrambling to find time for them further on. In fact, one of the reasons many people rarely take a vacation is because they never plan for it. Taking an accurate inventory of your current activities is the essential second step in the process of assessing your situation. Be completely honest here. Don't leave anything out—even the unplanned but persistent activities such as television watching and long phone conversations, especially if they account for noteworthy chunks of time during your day. I have made a list of common activities below to help you get started. Check the ones that apply to you and add any others that apply to you that are not on this list. To the right of each item, note the amount of time you spend on that activity.

Work
☐ Preparing for work

☐ Daily commute (round trip)

☐ After-work events

☐ Responding to messages on your BlackBerry

☐ Traveling to appointments

☐ Working and being at work

☐ Working on projects after hours

☐ ....

- ☐ ....
- ☐ ....
- ☐ ....

Relationships

- ☐ Time with yourself
- ☐ Time with spouse or significant other
- ☐ Time with children
- ☐ Time with family
- ☐ Time with friends
- ☐ Social events
- ☐ ....
- ☐ ....
- ☐ ....
- ☐ ....

Finances

- ☐ Paying bills
- ☐ Tracking down missing bills, paying bills late, or talking to creditors
- ☐ Shopping for items paid for with a credit card whose balance will not be paid in full when the statement arrives
- ☐ Worrying about money
- ☐ Planning, reading, or educating yourself about money
- ☐ ....
- ☐ ....
- ☐ ....
- ☐ ....

Health, Living, and Physical Environments

☐ Cooking

☐ Exercising

☐ Eating breakfast

☐ Eating lunch

☐ Eating dinner

☐ Organizing and/or cleaning

☐ ....

☐ ....

☐ ....

☐ ....

Spiritual Life

☐ Praying or meditating

☐ Engaging in joyful activities that bring you peace and happiness

☐ Attending a worship service

☐ Reading inspirational books or listening to uplifting music

☐ ....

☐ ....

☐ ....

☐ ....

STEP 3: MODEL

There is an old Japanese saying: Vision without action is a day-dream. Action without vision is a nightmare. Many people are too busy because they've taken action, accepted responsibilities, and said "yes" to too many requests before creating a vision for what they want their life to look like. Consistent action without a vision is a busyness nightmare. If you really want to take control of your life, you need a model for where you are headed. Your model can be a role model that you observe or an ideal that you imagine.

Now it's time to dream! Your model is the ideal that you are aiming for over the course of these 28 days—and beyond. So close your eyes for a moment. Take a deep cleansing breath. Smile. Now imagine yourself in your ideal life—a life with the space to accomplish the things that truly matter to you and one that alleviates the time-wasters that bear no fruit in your life. What activities would you engage in on a daily basis? How about weekly? Monthly? What would you do once a year? Make some notes on the following pages and give yourself free reign to dream big and listen to your heart's deepest desires.

Daily

Work

....
....
....
....

Relationships

....
....
....
....

Finances

....
....
....
....

Health and Physical Environments

....
....
....
....

Spiritual Life

....
....
....
....

Weekly

Work

....
....
....
....

Relationships

....
....
....
....

Finances

....
....
....
....

Health and Physical Environments

....
....
....
....

Spiritual Life

....
....
....
....

Monthly

Work

....
....
....
....

Relationships

....
....
....
....

Finances

....
....
....
....

Health and Physical Environments

....
....
....
....

Spiritual Life

....
....
....
....

Annually

Work

....
....
....
....

Relationships

....
....
....
....

Finances

....
....
....
....

Health and Physical Environments

....
....
....
....

Spiritual Life

....
....
....
....

Now, what activities would you need to eliminate in order to make space for this model to emerge in your life?

Work

....
....
....
....

Relationships

....
....
....
....

Finances

....
....
....
....

Health and Physical Environments

....
....
....
....

Spiritual Life

....
....
....
....

A New Declaration

I would like to challenge you with a personal declaration to aspire to, based on the Ten Commandments of Self-Care that I presented in the introduction. Perhaps the model you created mirrors the vision below, or perhaps the vision below is a stretch. These are practical, simple ways to know that you are effectively making a lifestyle shift from busyness to self-care.

DECLARATION OF MY PERSONAL LIFESTYLE

1. I only engage in activities that reflect what really matters to me.
2. I take all of my vacation time every year.
3. I make a heart-to-heart connection every day with someone I care about.
4. I honor my body's need for rest.
5. I have fun at least once a week.
6. I eat at regular intervals and at a slow pace.
7. I find enjoyable ways to exercise at least three times per week.
8. I do not allow technology to consume my time, but use it to maximize my time.
9. I say no to activities that do not pass my "personal priority test."
10. I listen to my inner voice when making decisions.

In the days to come we will address all ten of these declarations, and you will begin to embody each one of them.

My Challenge to You Today

Over the next twenty-four hours, take note of every activity for which you cannot satisfactorily answer the question, "What's the purpose of this?" Open your mind to the possibility of eliminating it from your life. You don't necessarily have to eliminate each of them today, but open the door to the possibility that if it doesn't serve a meaningful purpose, it isn't worthy of your time.

Five-Minute Journal

What does your ideal day look like? What would it take to manifest this ideal day in your life?

One-Minute Meditation

Meditate on the vision you wrote today. Close your eyes and picture yourself there. Make a declaration to yourself to take steps forward until you arrive at your vision.

DAY 3

Hurrying Up Is
Slowing You Down

Some days I feel like I'm running to keep up, but I'm
on a treadmill so I'm not really going anywhere.
That's when I know it's time to take a break and get
clear on my priorities.

—DAN, 35

It occurs to me that you may have read the subtitle of this book
and concluded that you don't really need 28 whole days to make
your shift. You can breeze through this program in ten—maybe
even seven. If the thought crossed your mind that you can get
through it quickly or that you simply may not have time to
spend 28 days gaining control of your schedule, this chapter is
especially perfect for you. Even if you are reading the book
straight through, do so with the intention of beginning the plan
after you finish the book. Just begin again at Day 1 and go
through the challenges one day at a time the second time
through. When you rush through anything, you risk missing
important details. I have discovered that all too often, hurrying
actually slows you down. Let me share an example from my
own life.

Pay Attention to the Details

Have you ever done anything so dumb you never even bothered to tell anybody about it? Well, for the sake of sharing a life-enriching lesson, I'm going to share a little adventure I had this week that certainly fits the bill. On Monday morning I packed up and headed to Baltimore-Washington International Airport to fly to Dallas for several public appearances. I accidentally took the wrong exit heading to the airport, but having left in plenty of time, I recovered. I thought that I had overcome the worst of my travel dilemmas, but it was only the beginning. I arrived at the airport and proceeded to check in at the airline kiosk.

After inputting my name, I saw a peculiar headline flash across the screen of the kiosk: "We have no record of your reservation." Hmm. That's odd, I thought, feeling confident that there was an error in the system. So I put in my flight number. I pressed the numbers 4-1-9-5 on the touch-screen's pretend keyboard. But my confidence wavered as I read the next headline on the screen: "There is no Flight 4195 that leaves from Baltimore. Please see an agent." I was sure I had the right flight number and the right airline. What could possibly be the problem?

I pulled out my itinerary to confirm the flight number, which I'd checked three times before leaving home. That's when I discovered the obvious detail I didn't check. My heart dropped to the pit of my stomach as four words that I hadn't noticed before now seemed to jump off the page: Washington Reagan National Airport. I was at the wrong airport! The flight was leaving in less than an hour and there was no way I'd make it. I felt like crying. I also felt like laughing.

"There's a flight leaving in four minutes from this airport, but the next one after that doesn't leave for six hours," the agent said apologetically. "Your best option is to drive to Reagan National and catch the next flight—you'll have to connect through Atlanta, though."

So, after driving fifty minutes to the wrong airport, I had to go back in the direction I'd come from to drive an hour to get to the right one. The right airport was actually just twenty minutes from home! *Good grief.* As I drove, I couldn't help but ponder a question: What lesson should I learn from this frustrating experience?

Asking, "What's the lesson in this?" can become a way of life that empowers you to make corrections and adjustments to make everyday life easier. Something as simple and avoidable as showing up at the wrong airport is more than just an aggravating mistake. It can serve as a wake-up call, if you will listen. What recent wake-up calls have you gotten? What was the message?

If you are open to learning the lessons in your everyday experiences, you will be less frustrated by life's aggravations and enlightened to avoid making the same mistakes repeatedly, especially the mistakes that are a result of constantly being in a rush. Here's what I learned:

1. Hurrying up slows you down.
If I had paid closer attention to my travel itinerary before I left, the entire fiasco could have been avoided. We typically think we are saving time by hurrying, but this is often not the case. Think of the times you've been cut off in traffic by someone who ends up sitting right next to you at a red light thirty seconds later. You can create the illusion that you are moving more quickly, but really, you are just using more energy and risking an accident in the process.

2. Pay closer attention to the details (even the details you think you have under control).

When you are used to doing something (in my case, traveling), it can be easy to take certain details for granted. Even when you think you know, double-check before you proceed with your plan. Many grand plans have failed because a small but critical detail was missed.

3. Don't sweat the small stuff.

Don't get worked up over issues, especially ones that can be resolved in some way. Be grateful for the lesson and the opportunity to bounce back from your mistakes. A major part of feeling stressed and overwhelmed is our reaction to the obstacles and setbacks we encounter. When you allow them to upset you, you create the illusion that life is more hectic than it actually needs to be. Choose to remain calm in the midst of a crisis.

4. Create a Plan B . . . fast!

You don't have time to sulk over errors. Instead, begin immediately focusing on the solution. What's done is done, but problems can get worse if you are slow to adjust to change so that you can accomplish your desired outcomes despite the obstacles you face.

5. Laugh at yourself.

You're only human, and we all make silly mistakes from time to time. When you do, lighten up a little, laugh a bit, and go with the flow. Laughter gives you perspective on life. I realized that even if I'd missed the opportunity to get to Dallas altogether, the world would not come to an end. It would be very disappointing, but trust that if something doesn't work out, perhaps it wasn't meant to be or something else will come along.

Throughout this book, you'll notice several illustrations that occur as a result of my travels—many of them tickling, some of them not. I think traveling is a metaphor for our journey through life. It is always more enjoyable when we can do it at a pace that is comfortable and relaxing. When we are not under a time crunch, the supposed hassles of travel—packing, going through security at the airport, delays, errors, and layovers—are no longer frustrating, but just a part of the process we go through to get to our destination.

What details do you need to pay closer attention to? Whether it's paying closer attention to your deadlines or brewing problems in a relationship; getting better organized; or keeping better track of your spending, a few extra moments can save you from making mistakes that cost you time, money, energy, and aggravation. All four of those—time, money, energy, and aggravation—can be negative consequences of an overextended life.

My Challenge to You Today

Slow down. Walk more slowly, talk more slowly, and drive the speed limit. Notice how it feels to move at a slower pace.

Five-Minute Journal

Consider your whole life—your work, finances, health, relationships, and spiritual life. What details have you been neglecting? What would you be willing to do to slow down and pay more attention to the details?

One-Minute Meditation

Hurrying slows me down. I choose to be more intentional about the pace of my life.

DAY 4

Busyness Is Often Based in Fear

I wasted too much time early in life and I've got to make up for it. That's why my life is so busy now. I work full-time, I'm raising two children, and I've gone back to graduate school. There's so much to do, but I feel like I'm constantly scrambling to make up for lost time.

—MELISSA, 38

As I have become happier, my desire to be "busy" has diminished. The word once held value and importance. As I more deeply fulfill my purpose on this earth, I have less desire to "do" more and a greater desire to "be" more. Perhaps you are noticing something similar in your own life. It can be a drug that suppresses pain you may not have even realized exists in your life. Busyness can serve as a distraction from our reality, including unfulfilling circumstances or broken relationships.

When I began to evaluate why my life was in such a state of busyness, I discovered one persistent emotion at the core of my drive: fear. I was in a hurry all the time because I feared that if I didn't stay ahead, I would lose ground. If I lost ground, then maybe I would discover that I wasn't as smart as I thought I was. Maybe I would lose opportunities. Perhaps I would lose my perception of who I was—someone who had been rewarded for her accomplishments, many of which had been based on doing things faster than everyone else. I joke with my mother that she had started it all by putting me in kindergarten a year early. I graduated high school early and finished college in three years. Subconsciously, I was hoping to prove to myself that I was smart after struggling academically during my first year of college. By twenty-one, I had a master's degree. I'd achieved my goal— early graduation—and assuaged my fear: I'm not dumb after all. But after crossing the finish line, it was on to the next thing— work. I never had time to enjoy the journey.

Of course, this only represents one type of fear. There are countless others that can drive you to overload and overdrive. If you are a parent, you may fear that if you don't involve your children in certain activities, they'll be deprived or held back in some way. If they don't go to a certain school, their opportunities will become limited. Even if you cannot afford it, you may make a choice to take on a more demanding job or a second job to increase your income to afford a better school district, private school, or other advantages for your children. Some people base their relationships on what they do for others, and therefore they fear the loss of love if they were to stop doing so much for everyone. Others fear that if they slow down and stop doing so much, they won't be needed. Maintaining an overload of activities helps them feel needed or important. They don't want to be replaced, so they carry an unbalanced burden of responsibility to demonstrate their value to others and themselves.

Why are you so busy? What are you afraid will happen if you slow down? If you can answer that question, you can get to the root of your fears and address them. Consider the following list of fears, and check the ones that resonate with you as a possible cause for your hurried pace:

☐ I am afraid things will fall apart.

☐ I am afraid of failure.

☐ I am afraid I will run out of time.

☐ I am afraid things won't be perfect.

☐ I am afraid of losing control.

☐ I am afraid of missing out on something.

☐ I am afraid to slow down because I will be forced to notice the reality of a difficult situation.

☐ I am afraid of what others might think.

☐ I am afraid I will be replaced.

☐ I am afraid I don't measure up and I'm trying to catch up.

☐ I am afraid I would be lost. I simply do not know any other way.

Driven by Fear

Fear can cause you to maintain a hectic, nonstop pace in multiple areas of your life. This kind of overdrive doesn't necessarily mean rushing around from place to place. There are multiple ways in which the overdrive syndrome can manifest itself in your life. Do any of these scenarios ring true for you?

MONEY

You charge things you just can't wait to buy. In a rush toward having what you want, it can be tempting to make poor financial choices.

WEIGHT LOSS

Rather than patiently adjusting your lifestyle to include consistent exercise and healthy eating habits, do you look for fast fixes to your weight problem? Pills, diet fads, and gimmicks are enticing.

SPIRITUAL LIFE

Does impatience cause you to push things forward without regard for divine timing? Sometimes it is simply impossible to know why things happen when they do and the way they do, but if you are patient, things often unfold in a better way than if you force a particular result.

RELATIONSHIPS

Do you rush into relationships and rush to move them to the "next level"? Out of a desire for companionship and love, you may be tempted to rush relationships—whether romantic or otherwise. But strong relationships are built over time. Time gives you the opportunity to learn about another person, determine your compatibility, and appreciate shared experiences. If a relationship is meant to last, there is no need to rush it.

WORK

Do you rush from one job to the next out of self-imposed pressure to get ahead? Climbing the corporate ladder and even building your dream business can put you on the fast track. Again, it's good to have a vision and goals, but treasure the process of getting to the vision as much as you do the vision itself.

Your Vision Can Create Fear

Having a clear vision of how you'd like your life to be can sometimes be difficult, especially when you simultaneously try to figure out how it will happen. When you don't know how it will all come together, the temptation is to limit your possibilities for fear that your vision will create problems in other areas of your life. For example, if your vision involves getting a less stressful job, but you have to figure out what the replacement job might be, thoughts of not having enough money, making a big mistake, or even losing your home can cloud your thinking.

Fear of Making a Big Change

Often, little changes are not enough. In this first week of your journey, it may be time to consider making some major changes. But major changes often generate fear. For some, that fear is intense. But the truth is that it often takes a drastic change in order for you to see any significant results. If fundamental aspects of your lifestyle—such as a job or a complicated relationship—are the cause of the majority of your stress and busyness, then it makes sense to reconsider those aspects of your life. Whether the issue is the length of your commute, a difficult boss, or the location of your residence, I invite you to allow yourself to feel the fear without treating it as a stop sign for change. Consider each of the following major changes. Would you be less stressed and more fulfilled if you implemented one of them?

- ☐ Move closer to work, thereby dramatically shortening your commute.
- ☐ Find a job closer to where you live, thereby dramatically shortening your commute.
- ☐ Work from home.
- ☐ Land a less demanding job.
- ☐ Resign your job to become a stay-at-home parent.
- ☐ Let go of one time-consuming activity in your life.
- ☐ Move to another city or state.
- ☐ Stop taking on more responsibility.
- ☐ Downsize your life—smaller home, fewer things (cars, boats, etc.).
- ☐ Downsize your expenses—get a less expensive house, car, lifestyle.
- ☐ Move to a less expensive city, where you can afford a less demanding job.
- ☐ Other ....
- ☐ Other ....

Which of the above ideas resonates most with you?

....
....
....

How would your life be different if you were able to successfully implement this change?

....
....
....

What would need to happen in order for you to make the change?

....

....

....

What scares you most about the idea of embracing this sort of change?

....

....

....

What is the worst thing that might happen if you made the change?

....

....

....

What is the best thing that might happen if you made the change?

....

....

....

Are you willing to try to make the change?

....

....

....

What would be your first step?

....

....

....

The series of questions above, if you answer them thoroughly and honestly, can serve as a self-coaching tool to help you decide whether a drastic change is needed. I believe you were drawn to this book for a reason. Our paths have crossed because it is time for you to shake things up. If the change that you sense in your heart is necessary is also a drastic one, I encourage you to embrace it. Expect that fear will be a part of the process, but refuse to allow it to stop you. I have often found that very often fear can be a sign that you are on the right path. A vision that doesn't evoke fear on some level is often too small for you. Dreaming big requires your willingness to step out on faith.

When my husband and I took a leap of faith to fulfill our dream of living in a place that would nourish us physically, spiritually, and personally, fear clouded my decision-making process. While my husband focused on the vision, I sometimes wavered. Our new house would be more expensive. "Should we be more conservative?" I asked myself. As I pondered my answer, I realized that making a financial decision that epitomizes your values—what is most important to you—is wise. Sometimes the emotional, physical, and relational value of what you get in exchange for your money is far greater than the money itself. That's when you know you are making a choice that will reap deeply rich rewards.

Even when I felt at peace with the decision, that didn't mean that fear would not show up from time to time. So I accepted it as a part of the process. And today I have absolutely no regrets.

I *love* my home, my community, and my city. It is priceless for me to be able to take a break in the middle of the day and stroll just a few blocks to historic downtown Annapolis, where I can walk on 350-year-old cobblestone streets and take in the charming views of Spa Creek and Chesapeake Bay. By moving, we dramatically enhanced the quality of our everyday lives and the joy we feel from living where we live. While my husband's commute is farther, he intentionally focused on creating the opportunity to work more from home. As a result, he goes into the office less often than before. And he is at peace with the sacrifice he made in order to make "living" a priority over "working."

As you make changes, big and small, accept fear as a part of the process. Then go for it! You'll never regret mustering up the courage to live the kind of life you've been dreaming of.

MY CHALLENGE TO YOU TODAY

Acknowledge your biggest fear. Make a decision to push through it.

FIVE-MINUTE JOURNAL

In what area(s) of your life do you find yourself rushing? Why are you rushing? What are you afraid will happen if you slow down? How can you address that fear?

ONE-MINUTE MEDITATION

Change is about choice. Fear is natural when I step outside of my comfort zone. I should expect it and keep on moving forward in spite of it.

DAY 5

Make a Heart-to-Heart Connection Daily

> I love my kids and we have a great time together.
> But now that they are teenagers, they are just as
> busy as I am. If we didn't live in the same house, I
> think I would hardly see them!
> —NEIL, 45

Once life becomes a series of nonstop projects, responsibilities, and activities to complete, it is almost inevitable that your relationships begin to suffer. Not only the quality of your relationships, but the quantity of meaningful relationships as well. A particularly busy executive, David, complained regularly of not having real friends. All of his time had been focused on his career for so long that he had no true friendships outside of his family—only acquaintances, colleagues, and clients. It was a lonely realization, but until he addressed the issues of his busy lifestyle, there was little he would be able to do about it. It's not just the career-minded who experience the loneliness of having few, if any, fulfilling relationships. Americans as a whole seem to have fewer close relationships. In fact, Americans' circle of confidants has shrunk dramatically in the past two decades. According to a study by sociologists at Duke University and the University of Arizona, the number of people who say they have no one with whom to discuss important matters more than doubled between 1985 and 2004.

Connecting in a meaningful way to the people who matter to you brings joy, solace, and fulfillment, especially in the midst of a hectic schedule. It allows you to feel grounded, knowing that despite the whirlwind of activity around you, there is something more important than all of it put together. Much of the emptiness that comes from being busy and overextended is a result of missed human connection.

Disconnection from Human Interaction

The continual increase in our ability to get what we want and be productive on the job and in life without interacting with other people has, in many ways, shifted our approach to interacting with one another as a whole. At times you may even find yourself aggravated when you have to talk to someone on the phone rather than pushing a few buttons on your telephone keypad or conducting a transaction with the click of a mouse. I recently heard a couple acknowledge that they often send one another e-mail messages while both of them are in the house together. Rather than talking, it is simply more convenient to communicate online. Little by little, the use of certain technology replaces human interaction. This is not all bad. Often it *is* much more efficient to use technology rather than have a conversation. However, when the habit starts to affect your relationships in such a way that it actually prohibits meaningful connection, it becomes a barrier. In what ways are you missing opportunities to connect with others because you are cut off by rushing, multitasking, or simply being exhausted?

Several years ago one of my friends had a habit of talking on her cell phone incessantly. To say the least, her multitasking had gotten out of hand. We would go out for brunch and she'd talk on the phone at the table. Standing in line at an event, she'd whip out her phone. Driving in the car, the phone would ring and she'd carry on a conversation about where we'd been while I sat there looking out the window waiting to continue the conversation we were having before the call interrupted. At first I didn't think much about it, but suddenly one day it began to bother me. I told her that I felt it was rude to carry on a conversation with someone somewhere else while a person in front of you is standing there. It defeats the purpose of getting together. She said she'd never thought of it like that and didn't mean to be rude. Although she didn't end her habit entirely, she improved dramatically and kept any extraneous conversations to a minimum.

Before the technology wave of the last decade or so, there were basic ground rules of personal communication. But with so many new conveniences, there are no ground rules. As a result, many of the habits that emerge from a fast-paced lifestyle are at odds with the concept of honoring one-on-one connection—something that, as you know, is the very foundation for a well-rounded, fulfilling life.

Make Time for Relationships When It Seems There Is None

Making a meaningful connection with the people you care about often means being proactive. If everyone is busy, there is no sense in sitting and waiting for one of the parties to make time for the other. It's not about blame or guilt. If you want to connect meaningfully, sometimes that means you have to be the one to step up and make it happen. If there is a loved one you haven't seen in a while, plan a way to get together. Call this person up to see when you can get on their calendar. Be open to their ideas of what they might like to do. Find ways to incorporate what you are already doing into an opportunity to spend time with someone else. One of my clients longed to spend more time with her adult children, who, of course, had their own full schedules. So she simply started demanding they make time for their mother—and it worked!

While interviewing authors Lois Evans and Priscilla Shirer, wife and daughter respectively of popular author and pastor Dr. Tony Evans, I asked how they managed to stay connected as a family. Dr. Evans, who can be heard daily on ninety radio stations around the country, leads a large congregation in Dallas that surely keeps his schedule quite full; Priscilla travels, speaking around the country thirty to forty times per year while raising two sons with her husband; and Mrs. Evans has three other adult children and six grandchildren. With spouses, there are fifteen people in all! So how do they do it? "The entire family has breakfast privately at the church every Sunday between services," Mrs. Evans explained. "This is our time as a family, and it ensures that everybody gets to see each other at least once a week." They worked together to find a way for their family to stay connected consistently. Even if everyone is "busy," their time for family is a priority.

Another friend mentioned how she was frustrated that her schedule limited her time with her teenage niece. She felt they were not as connected as they had been when her niece was little, and wanted to nurture that bond. So she decided to take her niece on a business trip overseas with her that summer. Not only was it a great learning experience, but the two became closer than ever and her niece gained a greater understanding and excitement for her aunt's work. Sometimes it is necessary to be creative in order to build and sustain your most important relationships. You cannot simply expect closeness to happen automatically. You must make the time and create the circumstances under which a relationship can flourish.

What are some ways you could create opportunities to connect with those who are a top priority in your life? How can you incorporate them into your existing activities? List three ways here.

1..

2..

3..

Whether you are surrounded by family or in a romantic relationship, or are in a new city and know very few people, here are some simple ways you can reach out to others and make a heart-to-heart connection. Here are seven habits for connecting daily:

1. Engage in stimulating conversations.
When your pace is hurried, quality conversations can be rare. One of our favorite questions at the end of the day in my house is, "What's the best thing that happened to you today?" It beats "How was your day?" any day. Stimulating conversations are ones that spark dialogue, meaningful interaction, and even reflection. Refuse to allow your conversations to become routine. Listen to what's going on with each person with whom you want to connect. Be genuinely interested and your conversations will naturally be stimulating.

2. Reach out and touch.

Diana Ross sang, "Reach out and touch somebody's hand. Make this world a better place if you can." It may sound cliché, but it's true. Nurturing touch makes your world a better place. Touch is healthy, nourishing, and an essential element of connection. If you do not live alone, you should hug or kiss (or both) every loved one in your house on a daily basis. Your spouse and children should feel your affection. Even if you are not a "touchy feely" kind of person, aim for at least one hug or one kiss per day. Another important way to touch others is by simply focusing on them. Look into the person's eyes. Stop what you are doing and give them your full attention. Because most listeners are being pulled in multiple directions, many people do not have a daily experience in which someone gives them their full attention while talking to them.

3. Help someone in need.

When you are juggling multiple responsibilities, it can be easy to feel like you don't have time to help others. The truth is that we cannot afford *not* to help those in need. There are so many people in the world who would love to have your problems. They'd trade with you in a heartbeat. Helping someone in need puts your life and your level of busyness in perspective. It grounds you and inspires gratitude while empowering you to make a difference.

4. Acknowledge people for who they are more than for what they do.

When you acknowledge someone for who they are, you notice the character traits or sacrifices that were required in order for them to do certain things. Whether it is a coworker, friend, or family member, when they do something well, acknowledge what it took for them to do it. Rather than a simple "Good job," you can connect heart-to-heart by saying, "It took a lot of patience for you to deal with that situation, but you did it. That says a lot about you." Rather than, "I'm proud of you for getting good grades this semester," you can say, "It took a lot of discipline and perseverance for you to earn these grades. You are excellent." Being acknowledged for who you are is a good feeling, and as long as your words are true, it helps build an authentic connection.

5. Laugh.

Another way to connect is to lighten up and laugh. When you become too busy, it can be easy to simultaneously become too serious. Connect heart-to-heart with others by sharing a laugh together.

6. Journal.

Making a heart-to-heart connection with yourself is the first step to making an authentic connection with others. One way to connect daily is to take a few moments to reflect. This is one of the reasons a journaling assignment (your Five-Minute Journal) is a part of the daily habits in the 28-day plan.

7. Meditate.

Just as you may sometimes talk to people without connecting with them (I call it talking "at" them), you can meditate with the same approach. Meditation is all about being quiet and *listening*. Listening—rather than hearing—is about understanding what you hear and taking action based upon it. Begin your meditation by giving thanks; express gratitude for the gifts of life, wisdom, and love. Then communicate your desires and needs. Make it a point to quiet down regularly to meditate, maximize your concentration, glean wisdom, and nourish your spirit.

My Challenge to You Today

Connect heart-to-heart with those you encounter.

Five-Minute Journal

What important relationships in your life are lacking a consistent heart-to-heart connection? What could you do to change that? When will you begin?

One-Minute Meditation

A heart-to-heart connection is the key to building fulfilling relationships. I commit myself to connecting daily with those who matter most to me.

DAY 6

Work to Live,
Don't Live to Work

> I feel pressured to work late because it makes me appear dedicated. Sometimes I spend Sundays preparing for the workweek so that I can hopefully have a head start on Monday mornings. It works well, but I resent not having my weekends and evenings all to myself and my family.
>
> —LAURA, 39

A 2006 *Time* magazine article asked, "Why do Americans have to work so hard at taking it easy?" Americans take less vacation time than any other people in the world. According to the Bureau of Labor Statistics, 25 percent of Americans receive no paid vacation time. Compared with other industrialized nations, we are allotted fewer vacation days—14 days on average, while British workers get 24 days per year, on average, and the French get 39 days. That's six to eight weeks! But despite the paltry amount of time we are given for vacation, we still struggle to find the time to take it! Many people feel so pressured by the everyday demands of life that they are exhausted, struggling to keep pace and dreading the work that piles up when they choose to take a break. The average worker has four unused vacation days left over at the end of the year. The Conference Board, a private research group, found that as the summer started in May 2006, 60 percent of Americans had no plans to take a vacation over the next six months.

There are a few reasons that most people give for not taking time off. One of the main reasons is the fear of being overwhelmed and stressed upon returning to work to a flood of messages, an overloaded in-box, and missed productivity. Others fear the appearance of not being committed to the job. For some, having "face-time" in the office supersedes having downtime in one's personal life. Still for others, it is a simple matter of putting work before all else. These attitudes and fears don't show up just in the ways many people spend (or don't spend) their vacation time, but in how they spend any of their time that should be reserved for personal life. A handful of companies, such as PricewaterhouseCoopers, shut down altogether one to two times per year to ensure that workers get some time off without the stress of worrying about all the work piling up while they're gone. But for now such policies are implemented at a small minority of companies.

When your life revolves around work, your whole life is out of balance. There is a big difference between working to live and living to work. When you work to live, work serves you. It fulfills a calling or passion. It provides resources that allow you to meet your basic needs and hopefully create the kind of life you want to live. It is just one piece of a larger pie that comprises your life's hours and priorities. But because work often demands so many of our waking hours, it naturally demands more of our attention. It takes on a level of social and emotional importance that can create imbalance and unhappiness. Today, I invite you to ponder the distinction between "living to work" and "working to live."

Living to Work

Melissa is a single, successful management consultant who worked her way up to senior management in a consulting firm by the time she was twenty-nine. She then pursued her longtime dream of launching her own business. Within a few years, business was consistent and booming. The problem was that it was consuming her life. She didn't seem to notice it until friends began calling her less, and a couple of them made snide remarks every time she would bring up work, which was often. Finally, a true friend she'd known since childhood told her the truth. She was just too wrapped up in her work. She'd become boring. Every conversation seemed to circle around talking about projects, travel, and her goals for the business. Her friends were happy for her, but they were exhausted by her relentless focus on her job.

Melissa knew they were right. They missed their multidimensional friend who had lots of different enthusiasms and took a genuine interest in their lives. As much as she hated to admit it, she really didn't have much of a personal life anymore, and it had become hard to remember who she was without her job or her company. Since she loved her work and business so much, she poured everything into it—to the detriment of her relationships with friends and family. It took some time to readjust her attitude, but over time she began to find a balance.

Most important, she enjoyed this newfound freedom in which her identity was not so intertwined with what she did for a living. It was a freedom that empowered her to take time off without guilt, spend more time with friends, take restful vacations, and reignite her love life. Interestingly, she began attracting better professional opportunities, too! In the process of finding balance, she had become more attractive—both personally and professionally.

To determine if you are working too much, consider your responses to these statements:

- *You talk about work more than any other topic.*
- *Your work often replaces time with friends and social outings.*
- *Your home is a second office.*
- *You consistently work overtime, whether there is a pressing deadline or not.*
- *You take work, and even your laptop or handheld computer, with you on trips (such as a family reunion, vacation, weekend trip, etc.).*
- *Work provides more joy in your life than anything else.*
- *You feel that sleep and personal time cut into your work time.*
- *The last time you took vacation time was more than six months ago.*

Working to Live

Working to live embodies the personal declarations you read and proclaimed for yourself on Day 2. Let's further explore some practical ways that you can make this shift:

1. Take all of your vacation days every year.
If you are self-employed, write a contract with yourself for your vacation and personal time—just as you would with any other employer. Decide how much vacation time you will receive each year, then block out dates that you plan to take off. If you are a stay-at-home parent, you also get vacation time. You need it. Working an unpaid position should not preclude you from getting to take a vacation. Plan for it and make the necessary

arrangements to take time off from your normal routine to relax and rejuvenate.

2. Commit your off time to your personal life.

Your off time needs to be *yours*. That includes your breaks during the day, lunch hour, days off, vacations, and especially your time after hours. The average American takes about thirty minutes for lunch, and many eat right at their desks. In order to create a self-care lifestyle, it is vitally important to set boundaries around your personal time. Get away from your office during the day—walk out of your work area, leave the office, or take a walk outside. A change of scenery can do wonders for your energy. And when you are "off" work, immerse yourself in the things that are important to you *personally*. Set boundaries that empower you to leave your work at work—figuratively and literally. Having a fulfilling life means enjoying your work, but also enjoying other aspects of life just as much. There will always be more work you could do. It is important to recognize that your personal life wants and deserves just as much of your attention. Even if you don't have something specific to do, refuse to allow your work to crowd your personal space.

3. Take your rest seriously.

Just as the lunch hour has become shorter and vacations have shrunk, the amount of time Americans sleep has decreased steadily over the last century. In the late 1800s, the average adult slept ten hours per night. By today's standards, that sounds ridiculous. But consider that the average home had no electricity, so people's natural sleep patterns reflected the hours of daylight and darkness. As electricity became commonplace in the American home, the average number of sleeping hours dropped. Today, as activities and workloads increase, the average amount of sleep continues to decrease. Although studies show that adults need about 8.1 hours of sleep per night, the average person gets just 6.9 hours of sleep now. It is essential that you take your sleep seriously.

4. Plan your work around your life.

This sounds like a luxury to some, but it shouldn't be. Your work should serve your life. If it doesn't, then begin by planning your work around what is most important to you. For example, one of the reasons I love coaching and writing is that it allows me to set a schedule that is convenient for me and doesn't require me to commute to an office. As far back as age twenty, I recall aspiring to becoming an author because I wanted a fulfilling career but had no desire to meet the demands of a corporate position. I had a vision tucked away, and although I didn't think about the vision much, I manifested it because I set the intention. I planned my work around the kind of life I wanted to have.

5. Explore your personal passions.

What are your hobbies? What do you do that causes time to fly by? Incorporate your personal passions into your life on a regular basis. You don't have to be great at something to enjoy it. Explore interests that have always piqued your curiosity. Having a passion that is uniquely your own and empowers you to express the essence of who you are is an important ingredient in your self-care. It can add an element of anticipation to your life by giving you something pleasurable to look forward to regularly. It can also give you something to share with the people you love in your life. My husband's passion for boating, which he discovered when he bought his first boat three years before we married, has given us an opportunity to spend time together and with family and friends. Because boating season lasts only as long as it is warm outside, time on the boat is a focal point for us during the summer—and creates a haven of rest, rejuvenation, and fun. Whether it's gardening, boating, painting, fixing cars, singing, or anything else, identify and cultivate your hobbies or personal passions as an intentional way of filling your personal time with meaningful activities beyond your job or business.

6. Make your family a top priority.

Most people, if asked, will say that their family comes first. But it is your actions that tell the true story. Are you satisfied with the amount of time you spend with your loved ones? How about the quality of that time? Does work sometimes overshadow your time together or keep you from being present at family functions such as reunions, sporting events, graduations, and family gatherings? It can happen without you noticing it. Work becomes the excuse for not being able to participate in major milestones or even everyday activities. It can seem harmless until you realize one day that you haven't had a heart-to-heart conversation with your child, visited your parents, or called your sister the way you used to in ages. Make a decision today to put your family first. Make it a priority and work your work around it.

7. Live in a place that brings you joy.

Choose where you live based on criteria that you value most. For some, this means living near the office (although this can backfire if you change companies). For others, it means living in an area that is joyful to them, near family, or offers benefits that are personally meaningful. Working to live means that work funds your ability to live in a way that has special meaning to you. That doesn't mean it has to pay a lot financially, although that can be a positive reward of some career choices, but it means that it gives you the ability to live your values. When Crystal and her husband decided to move from Washington, DC, to North Carolina, their goal was to transition from "living to work" to "working to live." Each of them had great jobs earning more than they had imagined they would at thirty years old. But the days were long and the commute seemed even longer—an hour and fifteen minutes each way every day. The daily grind was wearing on them when it occurred to them that life could be different if they made some new choices. Crystal's family was from Raleigh, North Carolina, less than five hours away, and they both liked the city—especially the lighter traffic and less expensive housing. They wanted to start a family within a few years, and being near family would be a great support. With some planning and courage, they landed new jobs (and salary cuts) and moved to a place that offered a new kind of fulfillment.

My Challenge to You Today

Put your work into perspective. Refuse to allow it to overshadow or steal time from your personal life. Take a moment today to look at your calendar and block out your vacation time for the next twelve months.

Five-Minute Journal

Are you working to live or living to work? In what ways could you do a better job of planning your work around your life rather than the other way around?

One-Minute Meditation

Healthy relationships and self-care are a higher priority to me than overworking.

DAY : 7

Have Fun at Least Once a Week

> Some of my most joyous moments are playing with
> my nieces and nephews. It's like I'm a kid again!
> —DANA, 32

When you think of fun, what comes to mind? Perhaps it's the thrilling and the daring that you picture—riding a roller coaster, skydiving, or adventurous travel, for example. Those activities represent one type of fun. And it can indeed be fun to enjoy that kind of excitement. But for most people, that type of thrill isn't an everyday or even every week or every month kind of experience. Fun is less about the activity you choose than the feeling it gives you and the response it generates from you. If you want to create a fulfilling life, you must have some fun—at least once a week. Fun provides release, pleasure, and entertainment value. Here are some of the healthy and important benefits fun brings to your life:

- *Release of tension*
- *Exhilaration*
- *Laughter*

- *Freedom from time constraints*
- *Living in the moment*
- *Relief from the pressure to be right or do something right*
- *Liberation from issues that normally constrain you*

Those who live a balanced lifestyle recognize the immense value of lightening up and having some fun on a very regular basis. When was the last time you had some real fun? A friend of ours—we'll call him Jeff—had a hard time answering that question several years ago. He worked hard and was quite successful, but still felt as if there was nothing to look forward to on a regular basis. His was a classic case of all work and no play. His life was full of stuff to do, but none of it brought him excitement, joy, or delight. He liked his work somewhat, but there was a lot of it. So I guided him through a simple process to discover which activities might bring fun into his life. You can use this same process to identify your favorite fun activities. Ask yourself:

1. Which of the following do you want to experience on a regular basis when you engage in leisure activities? Check all that apply, then circle the top three.

☐ Happy   ☐ Successful

☐ Carefree   ☐ Peace

☐ Laughter   ☐ Exhilaration

☐ Thrills   ☐ Bliss

- ☐ Risk
- ☐ Competition

- ☐ Fantasy
- ☐ Quiet

- ☐ Exploration
- ☐ Calm

- ☐ Teamwork
- ☐ Adventure

- ☐ Excitement
- ☐ Challenge

- ☐ Elation
- ☐ Ease

- ☐ Triumph
- ☐ Growth

- ☐ Tranquil
- ☐ Connection

- ☐ Childlike

2. Engage your senses: Using the top three feelings you checked above, make a list of specific things you can see, hear, taste, and touch that will make you feel this way.

Feeling ....

   Sights ....

   Sounds ....

Tastes ....

Touch ....

Feeling ....

Sights ....

Sounds ....

Tastes ....

Touch ....

Feeling ....

Sights ....

Sounds ....

Tastes ....

Touch ....

3. What activities could bring me all of these things?

....

....

When Jeff went through this three-step process, it looked something like this:

1. How do I want to feel? Happy.

2. What things can I see, hear, and taste (he didn't answer for touch) that will give me the feeling of happiness that I want in my leisure time?

> Sights—*green trees, sunlight on the water, pretty girls*
>
> Hear—*good music, laughter, the sound of a revving engine (yes, he specifically named this as something that made him feel good!)*
>
> Taste—*good food, saltiness*

3. What activities would bring me the above things?

> *A walk in the park*
>
> *A show at a comedy club*
>
> *Being in touch with an old friend*
>
> *Enjoying a concert*
>
> *Everywhere I ever lived, I would go near the water for self-reflection. So being near or on the water with friends and good music on a warm day is the ideal!*

It probably comes as no surprise that Jeff is now a fellow boater. He had never previously considered taking up boating as a hobby until he went through the "sights-sounds-tastes-touch" process that made it obvious that perhaps he should at least give it a try. He says that discovering this previously untapped passion changed his life and gave him a focus away from work and responsibility that is pure pleasure.

We all need something to look forward to. And it needs to be something that isn't about work or just getting things done. These 28 days are about creating structures that prevent your life from becoming overloaded and unbalanced—ensuring that it is joyful, passionate, and purposeful. So fun has to be a part of that plan. What's fun to you? What have you wanted to do, but put it off until you had everything else completed? What if you made "fun" just as much a priority as those other activities? Then you wouldn't have to put it off. It's also likely that by taking your mind off of serious matters for a while, you'll be more productive with the other things you want to accomplish. You would be happier and your attitude would be better.

Fun for me is different from week to week. Some kinds of fun are planned months in advance—a concert or special trip, for example. Other activities are spontaneous times with friends, enjoying a hobby, or playing a game. Whether you're a daredevil or the type who enjoys gardening in your own backyard, begin making it a priority to incorporate fun into your life. I've simply asked you to have fun at least once a week, but in an ideal world fun can be a part of your everyday life.

Have you ever known someone who seems to have fun no matter what they are doing? It's all in your approach to life. It's in the way you interact with the people around you or how you engage in your work. When you are fully engaged in the moment, joy is bound to be present. And where joy is present, fun often follows.

Joy and fun can be related, but they are not one and the same. Joy is an inner state of being, a spirit of gratitude, an attitude of wonder, and an approach to life that unearths the good in every circumstance. As a state of being, joy is ongoing. You can have a deep sense of joy even when you are enduring challenging times. Fun, on the other hand, is enjoyment right now. It's a release, an ignition of excitement and pleasure for a specific period.

A while back, a coaching client shared a list of goals with me. At the end of her list of financial, family, career, and health goals, she mentioned a category she simply calls "fun goals." Although I plan fun things, I had never considered it as a separate category. But I have since learned the value in planning your fun just as you plan all of the more serious goals that make up your vision for your life. So my question for you today is one for you to ponder and play with: What are your fun goals?

Here are a few ideas to get you started:

1. Have fun goals for every week, month, and year (or whatever time frame suits you best).
Life can become hectic, routine, and mundane if you aren't intentional about doing things you love and enjoy. Create fun things to look forward to on a consistent basis. The annual fun goal may be something that takes more planning and time than the kinds of things you do on a weekly basis.

2. Choose goals that make you smile, laugh, or get excited.
Close your eyes for a moment. Take a deep breath and let it out as slowly as you can. Now . . . what excites you or makes you smile and have a good time? What fun have you thought about having, but haven't done in a while or at all? Make a list—just for fun.

3. Choose what you really want to do, not what you think you "should" do.
Having fun is about what makes your heart merry. Let go of ideas that are appealing to others but not that exciting to you. This doesn't mean that you should not do things with others that are fun for them. It simply means that you should also have activities in your life that are fun FOR YOU.

4. Don't make it complicated.

You can have fun in the simplest ways. Don't make your goals cumbersome or complicated. If you do, they won't be much fun, will they?

5. Keep a "fun file."

I created a file in my desk that's labeled "fun." Anytime an idea for something I'd like to do comes to mind or crosses my path, I put it in the fun file. Perhaps for you, it's a fun bowl. Write your fun ideas on little pieces of paper, then fold them and put them in a basket or bowl. When the time comes, reach in, pull one out, and go enjoy yourself.

How about your lifelong fun goals? In addition to things you may want to do once a week, go a step further and dream about the fun things you'd like to do in your lifetime. These are the adventures, thrills, and trips you'd like to experience. They take planning but create lasting memories and add richness to your journey.

My Challenge to You Today

Do something today purely for the fun of it.

Five-Minute Journal

What kinds of things would you like to do to enjoy more fun? What's kept you from having fun in the past? What could you do to make more room for fun in your life?

One-Minute Meditation

Fun is an important part of my life.

DAY  8

Take Stock of Your Self-Care Habits

> I love my "me time" and I'm working on enjoying more of it!
>
> —ANGEL, 42

Over the last week we have been laying the groundwork for your new lifestyle. I call it a self-care lifestyle. As you begin Week 2, let's delve deeper into the concept of "self-care."

Why Should I Aspire to a Self-Care Lifestyle?

At their essence, most people desire to live a self-care lifestyle. They may not have identified it in those terms, but they want it. The reason so many people are not living it is because they do not know how. They've been taught how to be busy, how to eat poorly, how to chase money and jobs, how to "manage stress" but not how to eliminate it, and how to overwork. What we are not taught is how to live well.

Consider the following mantra to remember why a self-care lifestyle is essential:

Your Mind wants a balance.

Your Body wants health.

Your Spirit wants peace.

Let's consider what each of these statements means. "Your mind wants balance" means that your mind wants to be challenged and stimulated, but it also wants a break from work and excitement. "Your body wants health" means that your body longs for you to treat it well so that it can operate at its optimal level for as long as possible. "Your spirit wants peace" means that at your core, you desire to live your life in alignment with who you were created to be. Your spirit wants to fulfill its purpose, to love and be loved, and conquer fear in all its forms.

If you can remember these three things and give them to yourself every day, no matter how much activity is happening in your life, you will create a self-care lifestyle.

Self-Care Test

Under each of the ten self-care categories, check every statement that truthfully describes you:

Health

☐ I have had an annual physical exam regularly for the last five years.

☐ I drink water daily, approximately half my body weight in ounces.

☐ I exercise at least three times per week for at least thirty minutes.

☐ I do not smoke at all, drink alcohol excessively, take illegal drugs, or have an eating disorder or food addiction.

- [ ] I currently eat at least five servings of fresh fruit and vegetables daily.

Spiritual Well-Being
- [ ] I love fully and freely in all of my close relationships.
- [ ] If I do not feel at peace about a decision, I do not move forward with it.
- [ ] I pray and meditate consistently.
- [ ] I fully use my gifts, talents, passion, and experiences to serve and make a positive difference in the world.
- [ ] I am kind, respectful, and loving to all who cross my path.

Emotional Well-Being
- [ ] I love my occupation.
- [ ] I feel loved.
- [ ] I have healed from past emotional wounds or I am currently getting professional help to work through my pain.
- [ ] I feel good about my accomplishments in life and I am not in a race to achieve more or make up for "lost time."
- [ ] I am fulfilled in every area of my life.

Relationships
- [ ] My relationships energize me.
- [ ] I am in a peaceful relationship with all of my family members.
- [ ] There are no issues from the past that keep me stuck from moving forward in relationships.
- [ ] I have no relationships in my life that drain my energy.
- [ ] My attitude enables me to enjoy my coworkers, customers, and/or staff.

Physical Environments

☐ I love being in my home—it makes me feel good.

☐ I feel safe, happy, and energized by the area in which I live.

☐ I do not have clutter in my home, workspace, or car.

☐ My work environment is not stressful or harmful to me.

☐ I regularly enjoy the outdoors.

Support

☐ I have the tools, assistance, and guidance needed to do my job with excellence.

☐ I do not feel overwhelmed by my chores and responsibilities, and when I do, I ask for and receive the help I need.

☐ In my work and my personal life, I have delegated everything that can be fairly delegated and do not hoard tasks for fear that others may not do as good a job.

☐ I am well-supported by my income (I could actually live on less than 75 percent of my income) and have a financial cushion for emergencies.

☐ I have mentors, advisers, and a trusted confidant who are available to talk when I am making important decisions.

Personal Appearance

☐ I feel confident and happy about how I look.

☐ My skin is healthy and smooth.

☐ I am very happy with the style and look of my hair.

☐ My nails are neat and healthy.

☐ My weight is at a healthy and attractive level.

Stress Elimination

- ☐ My job does not cause me ongoing stress.
- ☐ I am not stressed by my personal financial circumstances.
- ☐ I am not hiding, avoiding, or running from anything or anyone.
- ☐ My schedule could not be described as overloaded.
- ☐ I am never late or running behind on projects.

Time Protection

- ☐ I do not give in to pressure to say "yes" to activities I want to say "no" to.
- ☐ There are no activities on my calendar that drain my energy.
- ☐ I do not procrastinate—I either do what needs to be done or give myself permission to move on to something else.
- ☐ I am consistently productive and fruitful, moving toward my vision for my life.
- ☐ I do not spend time with any people I do not really want to be with.

Rest and Relaxation

- ☐ On average, I get eight hours of sleep every night.
- ☐ I have used my vacation time every year for at least the last two years in a row.
- ☐ I take a lunch break away from my work area every day.
- ☐ I do not work on my days off or after hours.
- ☐ I do not have difficulty sleeping or falling asleep consistently.

Shifting to a Self-Care Lifestyle

Making a permanent change in your life is a challenge, but it's possible. The key is to remember that shifting to a self-care lifestyle is a process. The habits that are not serving you well right now can be broken, but it will take consistency and perseverance on your part. That means that when you find yourself slipping back into a poor habit such as not eating well or getting enough rest, overworking or not connecting with the people who matter to you, don't be surprised! And don't beat yourself up about it. Just start again, replacing the poor habit with a good one. Eventually you'll revert to your old habits less often and your new habits will be the norm. Here are a few principles to remember as you shift to a self-care lifestyle:

1. Make a decision to change your lifestyle.
Every change you make begins with a decision. These 28 days are basically a series of decisions, followed by choices that support your decisions and make them reality.

2. Clarify what is no longer acceptable.
Shifting to a self-care lifestyle means that you are shifting *from* something else, presumably from a life of busyness. Make a list of what is unacceptable to you in your current lifestyle that must go in order for you to make the shift. For example, when I made the shift, I had to let go of my habit of working at night. As a self-employed person, I realized I had set no "office hours" for myself. The office didn't close until I was tired—or sometimes exhausted. What habit(s) will you have to let go of?

3. Clarify what makes you feel well cared for.
It isn't enough to identify what is not acceptable. I invite you to close your eyes and daydream about what makes you feel pam-

pered, cared for, and nourished emotionally, spiritually, and physically. Then write down all that comes to mind. Self-care is about what nourishes, maintains, and protects your mind, body, and spirit. What accomplishes that for you may differ from what it does for others. Tune in to what your personal brand of self-care needs to look like. Write it down.

4. Make self-care easy.

One of the reasons so many people do not engage in self-care consistently is that they have not set up their lives to maintain it. Consider the things that will make you feel nourished and well-cared-for on a daily and weekly basis. What would make self-care automatic for you? For example, are there appointments you could set on the same day of each week or each month that could be incorporated into your schedule? Could you remove the television from your bedroom to make it a more restful place? Could you put all of the items you need for a bubble bath in a basket right next to the tub so that next time you get the urge, it's no hassle? Take a moment right now to identify ways to make self-care easy and automatic for you.

5. Practice until it becomes a way of life.

Refuse to compromise on your self-care. When you begin making these changes, it is unlikely that you will do it perfectly right away. It takes time to undo old habits. And the reality of everyday life almost always threatens to infringe on your self-care efforts. At times you will feel like you are losing ground. We are all equipped with the knowledge of what we can do to take better care of ourselves and yet we don't always do it. But don't be hard on yourself. Just keep practicing until it becomes natural. For some, that may take a few weeks and for others the process can literally go on for a few years. The goal is not necessarily perfection, but progress. Give yourself credit for making progress.

6. Notice how much easier it is to do what needs to be done when you live a self-care lifestyle.

Incorporating self-care into your way of life gives you the energy and the foundation to better handle the challenges that come your way. One of the reasons so many people become burned out is because there is no cushion that softens the blows that can come from stressful situations, frustrations, and back-to-back activities. When there is a cushion, there is room to breathe and even enjoy all that you have to do. Life simply feels easier when self-care is a priority.

My Challenge to You Today

Make a decision to adopt a self-care lifestyle. From this lifestyle, you will automatically eliminate a lifestyle of busyness.

Five-Minute Journal

Review the ten elements of a self-care lifestyle from Day 2. Which element most needs your attention? What specifically do you need to do differently? How could you go about incorporating this change into your life? What support will you need? When will you begin?

One-Minute Meditation

Self-care is a way of life for me.

DAY 9

Develop a Self-Care Plan

> A little planning makes a big difference in my ability to find time for myself.
>
> —VICKI, 29

I have yet to encounter anyone who doesn't enjoy the way it feels to do something nourishing and energizing. During coaching sessions, clients always perk up when asked a self-care question. In the last chapter we talked about creating a self-care lifestyle and you determined where you stand in your self-care habits. Now comes the fun part—creating your personal self-care plan. What would you like to incorporate into your life that will maintain and protect your mind, body, and spirit? Close your eyes and imagine yourself feeling fully energized, rested, and healthy.

When Angela decided to get some support from a life coach, she was looking to improve her ability to manage her time. She didn't think she even had time for coaching sessions, but decided she could squeeze in two and a half hours per month to focus on reorganizing her life. One thing that became obvious right away—she was very hard on herself. She was asked at the end of her first session, "What would you like to do for yourself this week?" She replied, "I never ask myself that question. I've got so much to do, it seems like I'm holding my breath until I get it all done. And then I'll do something for me."

"Hmm. When do you think you'll get 'it' all done?" I asked her.

She laughed, "Well, probably never. So I guess I might as well add something for me into the mix." A smile crossed her face as she began pondering what she might like to do. "You know, I really need time for myself," she said. "And there are a lot of things I'd like to do, but just daydreaming about it feels good! This week, I think I'll take a bubble bath one night and a nap on Sunday afternoon," she decided.

I loved the conclusion Angela reached—she'll probably never live up to her expectations of doing everything there is to do, so she "might as well add something for me into the mix." Making your self-care as important as anything else on your schedule is essential to incorporating it consistently into your life.

There are ten major elements to an effective self-care plan:

1. Health
The first and most important element of your self-care is good health. Without your health, there is no need to worry about being busy because you won't have the option. People who live a self-care lifestyle know that being healthy is a top priority—and they make choices that are aligned with maintaining a healthy weight and good eating and exercise habits.

2. Spiritual Well-Being
Your spiritual well-being is about living your purpose in life, the strength of your faith, and your ability to love and be loved. No

matter your purpose in life, at its core, it is about you giving and receiving love. The purest test of your spiritual life is your ability to love others and accept love from others.

3. Emotional Well-Being
Emotional well-being is about how you feel about yourself and your connection to the world. Your emotions are your feelings. If you don't feel good about your life, if you have few people or things that add energy to your life rather than drain energy, your emotional well-being will not be satisfactory. A self-care lifestyle recognizes the importance of your emotional well-being in creating a fulfilling life.

4. Relationships
A self-care lifestyle places the importance of the people who matter most in your life before work, money, possessions, and status. Strong relationships are what enrich your life. While fleeting opportunities may sometimes attract your attention more than a relationship that could be taken for granted, your self-care depends in part on your ability to choose and maintain healthy relationships. Loving and being loved by the people who matter is what matters most in life. When you get to the end of your life, it is your relationships that you reflect on most. This is why we often hear of people making apologies and amends from their deathbeds. They aren't thinking about work and giving instructions about how to improve productivity or make more money. They are thinking about how they treated people and thanking those who loved and treated them well.

5. Physical Environments
Your level of self-care is reflected externally in your physical environment. The state of your emotional and spiritual well-being is often subconsciously reflected by the beauty and organization

or clutter and disarray of the three environments in which you spend the majority of your time—at home, at work, and in your car. Your environments can impact how you feel. This means that placing yourself in environments that inspire you can have a positive impact on your emotional and spiritual well-being. Conversely, environments in which the energy depresses or distracts you can have a negative impact. For example, I have written most of this book sitting on a comfy chair with my legs propped up on an ottoman surrounded by three large windows that frame a calming view of large, winding trees in my backyard and beyond. Even while you are working, self-care can be incorporated into your work style. Clutter and disorganization create the illusion that you are much busier than you are. A self-care lifestyle ensures that you are not unnecessarily encumbered by stressful distractions in your environment.

6. Support

If the goal of self-care is to nourish, maintain, and protect your mind, body, and spirit for the purpose of maximizing your effectiveness, happiness, and productivity, then it is essential that you get all of the support you can to help you do just that. Support may be as simple as delegating tasks to members of your family so that you are not doing everything yourself. This teaches others to learn to take responsibility for things that they benefit from, whether directly or indirectly. You may also need support in overcoming persistent challenges in your life, such as weight management, depression, or health problems. Don't hesitate to get expert help—from doctors, therapists, counselors, personal trainers, nutritionists, or others—when you need it. Taking care of yourself means acknowledging that you can't do or know everything—and that's okay. Seek out help. Support can also come in the form of paying for services you can afford to hire someone to handle for you on a regular basis—such as cutting the grass, cleaning the house, babysitting, doing your taxes, or doing your nails.

7. Personal Appearance

When you look good, you feel good. Being intentional about maintaining your personal appearance is not narcissistic, it's good self-care. It gives you confidence and often increases others' confidence in you, which can lead to purposeful opportunities to reach important goals, live your purpose, and step into your vision. When you are living a self-care lifestyle, you maintain a hairstyle and cut that suits you, wear clothes that fit and flatter you, and enjoy the weight benefits of exercising and eating well.

8. Stress Elimination

Notice this category is not called "stress management." I don't want you to focus on managing stress; I invite you to focus on eliminating it from your life. If you focus on stress elimination, you are bound to at least experience stress reduction. Stress management, on the other hand, implies that there must always be stress, so deal with it. Implicit in that attitude is permission to create and deal with stress that may be entirely unnecessary. I want you to get to the core of stress in your life and focus on eliminating the source of it. In working with a variety of coaching clients, I have often found that people are busy dealing with issues that are long overdue to be eliminated from their lives. Because it's always been there, they keep dealing with it. It's time to drop that approach. In the next chapter we'll talk about how.

9. Time Protection

Like stress management, I think "time management" is also a misnomer. We all get the same amount of time each day. It is perhaps the only resource in life that is distributed in equal amounts. But multiple opportunities, tasks, projects, relationships, and activities all want some of your time. You must protect the time you have from being consumed by activities that do not reap a return on investment that will lead you to the vision you described on Day 1. Time is like money. If you invest it well, your future will unfold in a way that brings you great joy. If you spend it haphazardly, you may later find that you don't have enough of it left to do the things that are most important. So protect your time carefully. In the days to come we will discuss specific ways to create your own personal priority test to determine when a particular activity is worthy of your time and when it is not.

10. Rest and Relaxation

The last but certainly not the least element of a self-care lifestyle is rest and relaxation. In a culture that values "doing" over "being," rest has come to be considered a luxury by many. But you do not have to buy into this way of thinking. Our bodies were meant to rest. We were not created to work and play without getting time to rest and relax. So if you think you don't have time, then there is only one answer: You must find a way to make it a nonnegotiable priority. This means you carve out a period of time and make a decision that it is for *rest* and will not be encumbered by distractions, deadlines, or projects. You'll get to everything else when your period of rest has ended. This applies whether you are on a two-week vacation or a two-minute break. If you don't protect your rest periods in this way, they will not be relaxing and will not accomplish their purpose—rejuvenation.

Your self-care plan doesn't need to be complicated. It simply needs to serve you. To get started, I invite you to create your own plan consisting of three easy, self-care "standards" or rules that you invent for yourself. These are structures you put in place to ensure that in the midst of handling the responsibilities of life, you take care of yourself. For example, Angela eventually wrote three standards that stretched her in new ways and, though simple, nourished her tremendously:

- *Eight hours of sleep per night is my standard.*
- *My day begins with meditation and reflection (no time requirement on this).*
- *I take a bubble bath at least every other night.*

Over the course of our conversations, Angela had realized that she yearned for more rest—and that she was a more pleasant, effective, attractive person when she got enough sleep. So sleep became her top self-care priority. Today she gives herself credit if she gets as little as seven hours, but her goal is eight hours. This was very difficult at first because it meant she needed to be in bed by 10:00 P.M. But she promised herself that if she went to bed late, she would get up later. Since getting up later than 6:00 A.M. usually caused problems for a variety of reasons, she started taking her bedtime more seriously. This also meant that others in her household had to respect her decision to get more rest, and they adjusted accordingly. Her husband even began going to bed earlier with her. And now, after her full night's rest, the first thing she does is spend a few moments meditating. By not giving herself a time limit for this practice, she is free to spend it however she feels led. And she decided to make baths her third rule because she noticed that baths made her feel pampered and forced her to slow her pace.

What three self-care standards would you like to set for your-self?

1 ....
2 ....
3 ....

My Challenge to You Today

Begin implementing your self-care plan. Choose one activity or goal to set for today to kick off your self-care regimen.

Five-Minute Journal

Besides your three self-care standards, what other acts of self-care do you desire to incorporate into your ongoing lifestyle?

One-Minute Meditation

Self-care is essential for my mental, spiritual, and physical well-being.

DAY 10

Tame Your Tech Habits

> I feel trapped by all of the technologies my company makes me carry. I spend a minimum of ninety minutes a day answering messages on my BlackBerry. It starts while I am getting dressed in the morning, continues on the train ride in, at lunch, the ride home . . . it never ends!
>
> —CAROL, 42

Twenty-five minutes ago, I logged into my e-mail to check something very specific—the amount I needed to write on a check for a gift I am buying. Someone e-mailed me the amount, but I did not remember how much it was. When I logged in, there was a new message, which I checked. That message contained a link of interest to me, so I clicked on the link and spent ten minutes reading an interesting news article about the passing of a prominent author I encountered at an event a year ago. I said a brief prayer for her husband and family. Then it occurred to me to log into a financial account to check the status of a transaction performed yesterday. After that, I decided to check my secondary e-mail account, answered two e-mails, and logged off the system. I opened Word to begin writing. That's when I remembered—I need to write a check for a gift I am buying, but I don't know the amount to write it for. . . . *Oh.*

The Perils of E-Mail

Even those of us who have rules and boundaries around our e-mail habits sometimes suffer the time-wasting behavior that inevitably tempts us via e-mail. And that's just the regular e-mail that affects you only when you sit down at your computer. IMs, BlackBerries, and text messaging present other challenges that complicate the already busy lifestyle. This issue will likely grow as technology continues to evolve and new, improved gadgets replace old ones. A recent *Wall Street Journal* article, "BlackBerry Orphans," lamented the intrusion of gadgets into families and the resentment it can cause from children who feel neglected and unheard. If you are going to overcome busyness and embrace a self-care lifestyle, you must gain control of your technology habits now.

A friend recently told me about a conversation with a coworker. The coworker was commenting on the middle-of-the-night e-mails he regularly receives from a client. She gets an idea and then sends a detailed message about it, sometimes giving explicit instructions about how to carry out the idea or asking for his feedback or insight. At first he didn't think much about the fact that these e-mails were sitting in his in-box when he first logged in in the morning. Then it occurred to him to begin noticing the time stamp on the messages. Frequently they were sent well after midnight, often around 3:00 A.M. He mustered up the courage to jokingly mention it to the client one day. Without embarrassment or hesitation, she divulged that she sleeps with her BlackBerry. That way, if she gets an idea in the middle of the night, she doesn't have to remember it. He asked,

"Why don't you just keep a pen and paper next to the bed so you can write it down?" She replied, "Because then I'd still have to remember to send the message later. It's easier to just sleep with my BlackBerry."

Perhaps it hasn't come to this extreme for you. Nonetheless, your schedule has probably been affected in some way by the technology you use. It can happen gradually—the pervasiveness of time-consuming technology into the previously tech-free areas of your life. It can leave you feeling that you cannot get away. At all times you are accessible—and expected to respond to people. With little downtime, the pressure mounts and the stress intensifies. Of course, you've picked up this book because you are at a point of personal evaluation. And that means you can acknowledge what is and is not working for you, and make some changes that will realistically work for you.

As certain technologies came into existence in the late 1980s and early 1990s, we frequently heard claims of how great they would be because they would ease the burden of work we have to do. And it's true. Many technologies have eased the burden of work—the work we *used* to do. As time was freed from tasks that used to require more hands-on work, the time saved was instantly swallowed up by new tasks to fill up all of that "extra" time. This phenomenon is not new. Consider some of the technologies that became commonplace in the early to mid-twentieth century—the automobile, washing machines and dryers, and the shower, for example. These are all great conveniences that few of us would consider giving up. As these conveniences became the norm for American households, our expectations of what could be accomplished in a day dramatically increased. If you had to walk or use a horse-drawn carriage as your primary means of transportation, you would work very close to home—and be less likely to move hundreds or thousands of miles from your family. When washing a few loads of laundry is an all-day affair, it limits the amount of time you have for work outside of the home. Life had to move at a slower pace in decades past because there was no other option.

We have rounded a corner in the history of our culture. Those of us living today live at a faster pace than any people who have ever lived on the face of the earth. And it is all because of our response to technology. Rather than being a tool that allows us to enjoy more time, technology has become a way to do more, and do it faster. As a result, our lives have become overloaded, and many of us have shifted into overdrive permanently just to keep up. We are being pushed farther than ever before, to absorb more information and accomplish more activities. In order to restore a sense of calm and peace in your life while simultaneously maintaining productivity, it is necessary to be aware of this tendency and to moderate the activity and speed of your life. In a few days we will talk about finding and tuning in to your natural rhythm. But for now it is important for you to manage and control the impact of your personal technology on your life. Are there any personal communication technologies that feel intrusive or beyond your control?

☐ Internet surfing

☐ Work e-mail

☐ Personal e-mail

☐ Cell phone calls

☐ Home phone calls

☐ Work phone calls

☐ Work voice mail

☐ Home voice mail

- ☐ Cell phone voice mail
- ☐ Text message device (such as a BlackBerry)
- ☐ Pager
- ☐ Television viewing or recording
- ☐ Online instant messaging
- ☐ Other ....

Responding Versus Reacting to Technology

The main reason many people feel consumed by the demands of e-mail, voice mail, cell phones, and the Internet is because they react to the demands rather than respond to them. The cell phone rings, so they answer it. An e-mail arrives in the in-box, so they immediately read it and feel compelled to answer it even when they don't have time at the moment to do so. These conveniences have an important place in our everyday lives, but there has never been a set of rules that explains how to manage them. So the key is to set rules for yourself that work for you—and follow them. By prioritizing what is important to you, you can weed out reactionary behavior that will distract you from more important pastimes. What are some examples of reacting to technology?

- *Answering the phone because it rings rather than answering it because it is convenient for you right now or will allow you to accomplish important priorities.*
- *Clicking on links online because you are curious, or aimlessly surfing from Web site to Web site rather than remaining focused on your objective for being online at the time.*

- *Leaving on the audible e-mail alert on your computer and checking your e-mail every time it rings rather than establishing set times throughout the day to check and respond.*

The challenge with e-mail and other instant information technology is not the technology itself. The problem is how we use it. Just like so many other advances over the years, it is easy to incorporate a technology into your everyday life without noticing the ways in which it alters other aspects of how you live. Without noticing, suddenly you are losing hours every day because of how you manage something that should be more of a tool than a distraction.

To take better control of how you use your personal technology, I recommend implementing these seven boundaries:

1. Make e-mail unobtrusive.
One of the most tempting distractions is the little e-mail message bell that sounds on some computers once a new message appears in an in-box. For many of us (perhaps you fit into this category) the suspense is too tempting. Just as you begin to concentrate, you are distracted. So, turn those audible features off.

2. Open and respond at specific times.
This takes discipline, but it works. Set specific times that you will check e-mail and give yourself a specified period of time in which to respond. Make it a point to scan your new messages and respond to the most urgent ones first. Identify "urgency" by your definition, not necessarily by whether the sender marked it urgent. As you've probably experienced, some people mark everything urgent, whether or not it actually is. It is important

to make the urgency assessment up front so that if you run short on time, you can come back to less urgent messages during your next e-mail session.

3. Set "no e-mail" periods.

There should be certain times in life when e-mail is simply prohibited because you need to focus on a project, enjoy your time off, or simply be more sociable. In our increasingly isolated world, e-mail can too often replace face-to-face and voice-to-voice conversation. And many words are better expressed with the personal touch. So create periods in which e-mail is off limits—after 8:00 P.M., Sunday afternoons, while on vacation, or while you are trying to focus on an important project, for example. You know the periods when you most need a break from it. So set them to match the lifestyle you are creating.

4. Have "no technology" periods.

It is important to have time to just unplug. Whether you're having dinner, enjoying company, just walking in the door, or resting, there are periods when a phone conversation, e-mail, or television interruption—no matter how brief—is an intrusion. You don't have to answer the phone just because it is ringing—whether at home or in the office. If other priorities take precedence, then you need to set boundaries that allow you to focus on them.

5. Respond in the moment.

When overwhelmed with e-mail—and even voice mail messages—it is tempting to handle what you can manage at that time. As you've probably experienced, that leaves you with a backlog of e-mails to respond to. Sometimes those messages become buried and never receive a timely response, or any response at all. So make it a rule to reply to messages in the moment whenever possible. With ones for which you need more information, at least acknowledge the message to the sender and let them know to check back with you at a later time for a full answer to their inquiry.

6. Delete the message once it has been handled.

Many people are electronic pack rats. Just like your Aunt Mary, who still has her prom dress from 1962 stored away in the attic. There's no use for it, but maybe, one day, she will want to look at it again. Never mind that there's a great picture of it in the photo album. The truth is that there is very little information that you cannot access again if needed. Keep your in-box as clutter-free as possible and it will free your mind from feeling bombarded by the sheer volume of old messages, creating a feeling that you have more on your plate than you actually do.

7. Tame your BlackBerry habit.

I am a firm believer in the idea that you teach others how to treat you. If coworkers, bosses, or clients know that you will answer a message at any hour of the day or night—and within two minutes—they will take full advantage. You will attract more requests, demands, and messages than ever.

Once you set your new technology boundaries, tell a friend who will hold you accountable. Remember, this is not about "not using" technology. It is about managing your use of it to maximize its benefit to you. Remember, technology can be a great help to you, but if you are not intentional about how you use it, it can overwhelm you and create more work. If you are intentional, you can take better control of your time and eliminate busyness that doesn't lead to productivity and joy in your everyday life.

My Challenge to You Today

Unplug from communication technology. Do a technology fast—no television, radio, or phone usage today, and no e-mail or text messages except during work hours.

Five-Minute Journal

What technologies are distracting me from what is most important or draining my time? How can I begin managing the technology so that it helps rather than hinders me?

One-Minute Meditation

I choose when and how I use technology. I respond to it. I don't react.

DAY : 11

Eat Good Food, Preferably Sitting Down

I eat breakfast while commuting, lunch at my desk, and grab dinner on the way home from work. I usually eat in front of the TV.

—Miranda, 29

I used to tease my mother for eating breakfast standing at the kitchen counter. It became such a weekday habit for her that she would sometimes cook breakfast on a Saturday morning, then stand at the counter while we ate at the kitchen table. Similarly, when asked to sit down, she'd insist, "Oh, I'm fine. I like to eat at the counter." When I began my first job at twenty-two, I was usually so focused on a project that I worked right through lunch. By the time it occurred to me to eat, it might be three or four in the afternoon. By then I was famished and exhausted. As a result, I now have a knack for spotting those who are so busy they skip meals. Every day we make choices from an ever-expanding menu, but we forget to choose to stop and give our bodies the fuel they need to keep going.

I'd been working with a successful corporate executive,

Renée, for several months, when it occurred to me to ask her during a session to describe her eating habits. Her schedule had become so full that her efforts to keep up were frantic.

"What do you eat for breakfast?" I asked her curiously.

She paused, then said, "Well, I don't eat at home. I take my son to school, and then sometime during the morning I'll eat a granola bar or some peanut butter and crackers."

"What time is it when you eat that?" I asked.

"On a good day, around ten o'clock," she said.

Our session started at three o'clock, and I wondered if she'd had lunch. "What did you have for lunch today?" I asked her.

"Oh, Valorie," she said. "You caught me. I haven't eaten lunch yet."

"Yet? Aren't you going home right after we hang up?"

"Yes," she admitted. "This is how it goes at least three days a week. Sometimes I just feel like there is so much going on that I can't slow down."

"And how do you feel?" I asked.

"I feel exasperated, worn out, and quite frankly, hungry."

"How would you like to feel instead?" I probed.

"I'd like to treat myself better," she admitted. "I'd like to feel like everyone else's needs aren't so much more important that I sacrifice something as basic as eating to make sure they get what they want."

By the end of our session Renée had made a simple new promise to herself—to eat regularly. I asked her to eat in the mornings with her son, for whom she prepared breakfast, and to schedule a break for lunch away from her desk. Within a week she came to the session excited about how much more energy she had. Interestingly, she noted that it really didn't take much extra time to sit down and eat. She simply had to make up her mind to do it. In the process, she felt less hurried throughout the day. And she admitted that no one else was pressuring her to work straight through lunch. It was all in her mind and her approach.

Eating is a chance for you to refuel, relax, and reconnect. It is an opportunity to give yourself the energy you need to make it through the day at your best. It is a chance to take a break from all that may be going on. And it is a chance to reconnect with yourself or important people in your life. Today, I invite you to adjust your eating habits so that your meals serve you in multiple ways:

- *Self-care*
- *Energy boost*
- *A needed break*
- *Connection with others*

A woman told me recently that if she could just take a pill in place of actually having to sit down and eat, she'd do it. She sometimes sees eating as just another to-do on her long list of things to accomplish in a day. A pill may not be available yet, but many Americans have opted for milk shakes and smoothies that replace lunch. In fact, smoothies have become so popular as a lunchtime replacement that Smoothie King, the chain of quick-service drinks, commissioned a survey of 18-to-54-year-olds about their lunchtime habits and found that a hectic lifestyle contributes to both skipped meals and unhealthy food choices. The national survey revealed that 43 percent of Americans view lunch as the least important meal to overall health, and it is the least favorite eating experience. In fact, a majority of Americans (58 percent) admit they will skip lunch altogether if too busy. Half of those surveyed also said that they "view lunch as an opportunity to merely grab a quick bite or keep working." Eighty-two percent regularly spend thirty minutes or less on lunch, and 43 percent spend just fifteen minutes or less on lunch. That's not a lot of time!

1. Take note of your current eating habits. Be honest!

One of my clients, Cameron, was frustrated because she had gradually but consistently gained weight over the past few years. She insisted she wasn't doing anything out of the ordinary and therefore didn't think there was anything for her to do differently except maybe add a little more exercise. Of course, exercise was a big piece of the puzzle, but it wasn't the only piece. As I began to ask her questions about her eating habits, she revealed that she was too busy to eat breakfast, often had dessert during lunch while taking clients out on her expense account, made a visit to the vending machine around four o'clock every day, and picked up Chinese takeout after leaving the office at seven a few nights a week. By the time she actually sat down to eat, it was nine or ten at night. Oh, and she drank wine with her takeout. It eased the tensions of the day and made it easier to go to sleep.

Working with many people over time as a coach, I've had quite a few clients who succeeded in their quest to become healthier despite a seeming lack of time to dedicate to it. But it always starts with an honest account of your habits. Cameron's busy lifestyle gave her little time to ponder her eating habits, and especially to find better alternatives. But by raising her awareness of the unhealthy habits she was engaging in, she could address each habit with a new, better habit that served her health in a positive way. So let's start by being honest: What are the bad eating habits you sometimes engage in?

2. Eating should not be optional.

I know this sounds basic. But when it comes to eating well, we have to start with the basics because those who have hectic schedules often overlook them! Do you skip meals in order to get things done? Do you skip dinner because you're simply too exhausted to cook—or worse yet, too exhausted to bother eating—and head for bed instead?

3. Make it easy to eat well.

Cameron turned her situation around by doing some things that she already knew would be good for her, but she simply had not previously made the commitment to them. She began eating breakfast. It was not elaborate, but it was healthy—a mix of fresh fruit and walnuts along with a glass of juice. It took about sixty seconds to prepare and less than five minutes to eat. She decided she could make time for it. Although she had lunch outside the office, on average, about three times a week, she decided she would eat dessert only once per week. To control the late-afternoon runs to the vending machine, she added "delicious, healthy office snacks" to her once-per-week grocery list. Her list included nuts, apples, clementines, and low-fat popcorn. This way she would be prepared when the urge came to buy one of the fattening candy bars or bags of chips. Do the same for yourself. Start by making a list of tasty, healthy snacks to keep on hand. Both at work and in the car, it's great to have snacks on hand so that you are not tempted to reach for an unhealthy sugar rush or stop by a fast-food restaurant.

4. Don't just eat, dine.

Eating can be such a pleasurable experience, but not on the run. A sure sign of busyness is eating in the car, standing up at the counter, or not even leaving your office. You deserve better than to eat at your desk while you work through lunch. So shift out of overdrive by practicing the art of dining. Try eating at your dining room table, by candlelight, with your "good china," and no television. You might even play a little music in the background to enhance the mood. If you are single with no children, dining can become a way to relax. Savor your food, enjoy every bite, and eat slowly. If you are married, have children, or live with other loved ones, bring back dinnertime. Dine together. This is a simple way to strengthen your connection with each other. Dinner becomes a gathering place, a place to check in with each other, communicate, share stories, and enjoy each other's company. But it doesn't have to be just dinner. My client Susan was frustrated at the lack of quality time she felt she was spending with her son. I knew she'd mentioned not having time to eat in the mornings, but ironically, she also mentioned fixing breakfast for her little boy. "Why don't you sit and eat breakfast with him?" I asked. Her initial reaction was to say, "I don't have time to stop and eat." But she immediately thought about it. It would probably be a ten-to-fifteen-minute meal—a small amount of time, but a terrific opportunity for consistent connection. She agreed to try it for a week to see how it went. In our next session, she beamed. "Making time at breakfast gets our day off to such a positive start. I feel like I'm taking control of my time. And last week, my son asked, 'Mommy, are we going to get to eat breakfast together *every* morning now? I like this.'" Allow eating to be an opportunity for you to slow down. Consider it not a functional chore, but a moment to be savored and shared.

5. Drink plenty of water.

We have all heard about the importance of drinking water. But still, few people drink enough of it. Water is your body's most important nutrient. The human body is approximately 70 percent water! Dehydration leads to poorer mental function, decreased physical performance, overheating, and stress to your kidneys, heart, and other organs.

6. Adjust the time that you eat.

In addition to resolving to eat three regular meals a day, Cameron also made a commitment to leave work before 6:00 P.M. every day. This enabled her to get home in time to eat dinner before 7:30. She was careful to cook when the mood struck and to buy takeout that was more healthful. Her new rule was no eating after eight. Over the next six months she lost twenty pounds. Just as important, making it a priority to eat breakfast and a healthy dinner at a reasonable hour also helped her slow down. She found herself being more productive at work because she was staying at the office an hour less than before. And she gained more confidence because she felt good about how she looked.

7. Give your body good fuel.

As active as you are, you can't run on empty—and you can't run on bad fuel. Fried foods, junk food, sugar-rich drinks, salty foods, and rich desserts are not the kinds of fuel you need to operate at your best level. Good self-care necessitates eating premium fuel—lots of fruits and vegetables, lean protein, whole grains, and unprocessed foods. You deserve to eat well, and it starts with your choices.

My Challenge to You Today

Do not eat on the run. Slow down, choose something healthy, and dine—either by yourself or with someone with whom you'd like to share good conversation.

Five-Minute Journal

What needs to improve about your eating habits? What could you do to make that improvement easy for you? When will you get started?

One-Minute Meditation

Eating is my opportunity to refuel, relax, and reconnect.

DAY : 12

Get Good Exercise, Preferably Standing Up

I'm in the sandwich generation. I have an eighty-year-old mom in a nursing home and an eleven-year-old daughter discovering life—and lots of work demands. I have no life except my coveted sixty minutes of exercise.

—MONICA, 48

I saw a television commercial the other day that advertised a device that would supposedly "work you out" while you sat around and watched television or worked on your computer or did anything besides work out. Fit young men and women in the commercial raved about how well it had created their perfect washboard abs. I was a bit suspicious, however. There are many things that technology has given us, but creating a machine to exercise for us is not one I am convinced of yet. In the last chapter I asked you to sit down and eat. Today, I am asking you to get up and exercise.

Did you know that your body is a gift? We have just one, but sometimes we act as though we can get a quick replacement if we ruin the one we have. Not true. This is the only body you'll ever have, and your job is care for it so that it serves you well and empowers you to do all that you were born to do. Taking great care of your body is an act of gratitude that only you can perform. It is a form of worship. It is your thanksgiving offering that says, "I appreciate this vessel I have been given and I do not take it for granted." Our bodies are quite fragile, but often we don't notice this fact until something goes wrong. And many times it is the stress of being overly busy that contributes to illness and self-neglect. People are often too busy to go to the doctor, too busy to schedule a routine physical, or so stressed that they manifest a multitude of physical symptoms.

In my busyness survey, over 55 percent of the respondents said they exercised for thirty minutes or more less than once per week; 39 percent admitted to exercising for thirty minutes less than once per month—meaning they essentially don't get any exercise. Despite these facts, many expressed a desire to exercise and an understanding of its benefits, but said they simply could not find the time. More than one-fifth said that not having time to exercise was the most stressful aspect of their schedule. Tricia, thirty, from California, wrote, "The demands of work, housekeeping, and an overbooked schedule lead to lack of time to exercise and take care of me. This is stressful and frustrating!"

Others who took part in the survey have found a way to find solace in exercise. Sharon, a forty-six-year-old single mom from Missouri, admits, "I go to the gym to exercise early in the morning to get some 'me time.' " I like her approach: Rather than focusing on the physical effort she would put forth during her workouts, she focused on the benefit of having some time to herself.

Good exercise gets your body moving, your heart pumping, and your blood flowing. So while I asked you to sit down to eat, I highly recommend you get up to exercise. Make your workouts active and fun. Here are seven strategies to get up and get moving—consistently:

1. Give yourself a range of success.

Remember a few chapters ago when we were delving into the topic of self-care, I said the goal is not necessarily perfection, but progress? The same holds true when it comes to your exercise regimen. While you might aim for six or seven days a week, give yourself credit for progress even if you make it only three days of a particular week. And if you're not exercising at all right now, start by adding a couple of hours of physical activity every weekend. Your goal should be three days a week minimum, but for now aim for the number that feels manageable and excites you.

2. Make it quick and convenient.

One of the reasons many people never get around to exercising is because they believe it will take too long. Typically the complaint sounds something like this: "If I must work out for an hour and it takes ten minutes to get there and ten minutes to come home—and I have to shower and change—then it's really a one-and-a-half to two-hour investment." Most of us don't have that much time to spare three to five times a week. So try aiming for thirty minutes. If the time or expense or environment of a gym does not appeal to you, identify your alternatives. Work out at home. Take a brisk thirty-minute walk around your neighborhood. Ride your bike or go inline skating. Use a workout DVD or follow along the same time each day with a fitness program on television. Try thirty minutes of swimming at a local pool, or nearby beach if you have one. You have options. The key is to find something that is convenient and fast so that it is not a burden to you to achieve your goal every week. Give yourself something to look forward to, but make it something easily doable in a short period of time.

3. Multitask when you exercise.

Nowhere else in these pages will I suggest multitasking. However, exercise is a wonderful opportunity to do it, especially if you dread working out. Exercise can become your opportunity to reconnect with yourself, listen to your favorite music, or even meditate. My client Ingrid was frustrated by her desire to lose weight and by her lack of motivation. She mentioned during coaching that she also desired to spend more time in meditation. She just never seemed to get around to it. "Is there a way you could combine the two?" I asked. "Actually, yes!" she said. I could see the lightbulb go on over her head. She used time on the treadmill and elliptical machines to meditate or listen to uplifting music, and soon she began looking forward to working out. Because there was a secondary benefit from the workout, the act of exercising became more appealing to her.

4. Take a class, form a group, or get a trainer.

Are you the type who will show up for an appointment, but fail to appear if you have to set the schedule yourself? If so, set an appointment to exercise by taking a class, partnering with someone else who is committed to exercising consistently, or even hiring a trainer if you can afford one. This approach allows you to partner with others and create a social connection, something some people find very helpful in staying motivated. Make it a family affair by having your child, spouse, or other family member join you.

5. Make a plan you'll actually follow.

It can be so tempting to come up with a big goal when it comes to exercise. But more often than not, this approach sets you up for failure. Instead, make a plan you know you can actually follow. Make it something easy and doable. Then work your way up to something more. By starting small, you build your confidence and consistency.

6. If you fail, try again.

"Success is the ability to move from failure to failure without losing your enthusiasm," Winston Churchill once said. It sounds simplistic because it is. Stop beating yourself up for what you didn't do yesterday, last week, or this morning. If you didn't exercise when you said you would, there is nothing to be gained by sulking over it. Be honest with yourself. Why didn't you do it last time like you said you would? How can you overcome that issue now? Then try again. Just get started. Sometimes that will mean mumbling and grumbling your way to the gym. It may mean bundling up if it's cold outside and you want to take a walk. Whatever the case, do what you need to do. This process is building your character, developing your sense of discipline, and literally and figuratively shaping your future.

7. Start your day with exercise.

Do you feel like your schedule is full, so why bother trying to squeeze in exercise around lunchtime or at the end of the day? By then you're likely to be engrossed in other activities, and exercise will interrupt the flow. Or worse yet, you'll be too tired. I have found that one of the easiest ways to get my workout in consistently is to get moving first thing in the morning. Before you go to bed, put your workout clothes, shoes, and a bottle of water right next to your alarm clock. Remind yourself before you drift off to sleep that the first thing you'll do when you get up is work out. When you wake up, slip on your workout gear and head out the door for a brisk walk, pop in your favorite workout tape, or find an open area in your house to do a few sets of your favorite exercises. While you're exercising, reflect on the day ahead. Use it as your planning time, quiet time, or "me" time. You'll have more energy all day.

My Challenge to You Today

Get moving! Take out your calendar and choose the time and days that are realistic for you to exercise at least a couple of times a week for thirty minutes. Then get started. You can start small, but start now.

Five-Minute Journal

What would be a realistic and doable plan for you in terms of exercise? What would you actually do three days a week for thirty minutes? What will consistent exercise give you that you don't have right now?

One-Minute Meditation

My body is a temple. I will treat it as the divine gift that it is.

DAY 13

Be Led by the Spirit

> I was feeling stuck, like I'd created this monster (my schedule) who had gotten a mind of his own and I couldn't control him. But that wasn't true. I knew in my heart that it was time for a change—a big change—and that's why I was feeling so uneasy. It was a divine nudge.
>
> —KELLY, 34

Often clients hire a coach to help them find answers. They sense it is time for a change but are afraid of making a wrong decision. What they often don't recognize is that I don't have their answers. They do. My job is helping them listen and encouraging them to trust what they hear.

Kenneth, a freelance writer and marketing consultant, sought coaching to help him find some balance in his life. He thought perhaps the fast-paced life in Los Angeles was taking a personal toll on him. He missed his family and friends on the East Coast—and dreaded the five-hour plane rides, which turned into eight-hour trips because of the three-hour time zone difference. Working alone, he regularly stayed up until midnight working on client projects, then logged on to e-mail within ten minutes of getting out of bed in the morning because many of his business associates were in New York and they had a three-hour head start on the day. Although he had quite a few acquaintances and a few friends, he lacked the deeper friendships he wanted. And most pressing, at thirty-six, he wanted companionship with someone other than his dog. But when would he find the time? And if he fell in love with the woman of his dreams, did he want to settle down and raise a family where he lived? The answer was "no." It was expensive enough living by himself, and he wanted to buy a single-family home, but the prices in his area were out of his reach. After mulling it over, Kenneth came up with a few options:

- *Hire more help so that he could delegate some of his projects and only have to provide oversight.*

- *Move his satellite office to Nashville, where he'd made a few friends and knew of two reliable professionals he could partner with on projects. With a satellite office, he could spend more time on the East Coast.*

- *Work hard to just stick with his original business plan and make it work out in Los Angeles. He'd have to get more disciplined about increasing fees, saving money, and working only until 6:00 P.M.*

As I listened to him, I could hear a burdensome tone in his voice as we described each of these options. It was as if he were coming up with options that created more work and didn't give him what he *really* wanted in terms of more freedom and time. He was holding back.

"In your ideal scenario, what would you choose to do?" I asked.

"I'd move on," he admitted. "The bottom line is that I feel in my spirit that it's time to move on. I believe there is a message for me in this heavy burden. Work is not meant to be a burden. My eight years here have been good in many ways, but I'm older now. I want more than just a great career. I want a great life. I want to move to Nashville, where the pace would be slower, but not too slow. I can still do entertainment-oriented work there, and as for the rest of my work, it's all virtual anyway. I don't think my clients care where I am. I guess it's me who's hung up on the perception of my location."

Eventually Kenneth decided to follow his heart. He took an exploratory trip to Nashville. Then three months later, he moved there. Now, two years later, his business is thriving, he lives in a spacious house and has friendly neighbors, his work schedule has been tamed, and he has a happy social life.

Is there a fundamental change you need to make in your life? A fundamental change is one major shift that will resolve multiple challenges. It's important to identify a fundamental change if it needs to be made because it will save you from making a lot of small, insufficient changes that don't really get to the core of your desires. Fundamental changes are bold. They mark turning points on your journey. Perhaps your busy lifestyle needs a fundamental change that will give you what you've been longing for.

A Spiritual Approach to Your Everyday Problems

Glenna had learned to accept her insomnia as a way of life. Unable to stay asleep through the night, she would wake up three to four times and spend a lot of time trying to count sheep so that she could fall back to sleep. Her doctor had prescribed medication, which seemed to help slightly for a few weeks, but then her restless sleep patterns reemerged. Her husband's loud snoring contributed to the problem, but it wasn't the cause. Anxiety and worry dominated her thoughts. While work issues were sometimes worrisome, it was mainly her ailing father's Alzheimer's disease that kept her up.

Her sleep problems had begun shortly after he came to live with them. She never knew what was going to happen next. Some days he behaved very normally; on other days he refused to take his medication or would wander out of the house unannounced, leaving the doors unlocked and his whereabouts unknown. Some days he seemed happy, but many days he was frustrated by the circumstance of having to rely on his daughter to live. This had been going on for nearly two years when she brought it up to me, hoping for some suggestions. My first reaction seemed a normal one—to think of solutions and remedies that might help her get to sleep:

- *Go to bed at the same time each night.*
- *Engage in a ritual that lulls you to sleep (such as reading).*
- *Turn off the television, or if your spouse insists on watching television, find an arrangement that doesn't intrude on your sleep.*
- *Don't exercise before going to bed since it stimulates the body, making it more difficult to fall asleep.*

Some of the suggestions were significant, as Glenna had no established bedtime routine. But while we were coaching, I had the distinct feeling that we were trying too hard to find a solution. In these types of moments, I always find my answer by dropping the intellectual approach and allowing a spiritual approach to surface.

"Have you meditated or prayed about it, Glenna?" I asked. Immediately, I heard a glimmer of hope in her voice. I knew she would be open to the question.

"No, actually, I haven't," she replied. "I've prayed about quite a few things lately—especially about my dad, but despite the fact that it feels like my biggest problem, it never occurred to me to pray about getting to sleep. That seems like such a basic part of life that it never dawned on me that I *could* pray about it."

"Why don't you give it a try," I encouraged her, sensing that it was something she would respond to. Glenna agreed to give it a go.

The following week we spoke again. Amazingly and excitedly, she shared how she had slept through every night that week. She prayed before sleeping, meditated, and slept peacefully. Little miracles can happen every day when we take time to listen for the answers we need.

Major changes often require you to tap into the divine wisdom that wants to lead and guide you toward the best your life has to offer. Slow down and quiet down enough to listen to that divine inner voice that speaks to you, guides, and calms you. Consider these seven keys to taking a spiritual approach to making a fundamental change in your life:

1. Trust your divine nudges.

I believe that all the answers you need in order to assuage your challenges with busyness are within you. To find those answers, you have to listen to the divine nudges in your spirit. Sometimes the divine nudges offer one- or two-word messages: "Relax." "Tomorrow." "Leave." "Stay." "Not yet." "It's okay." Sometimes a simple one-word nudge prompts a major change. At other times the divine nudges give you more detailed guidance, preparing you for a change that is to come. While writing in my journal in June 2002, a message in my spirit told me that I would move in a year and live near the water. I was in Dallas at the time and had not given any thought whatsoever to leaving. On June 21 of the following year, I married, and on July 4, I moved to Maryland, where we lived near the water. The divine nudge prepared me for what was to come. When you feel spiritually led to make a major change, don't resist the message or ignore it. Trust it, even if it doesn't make sense to you right now. There is a greater plan for your life that incorporates more joy and fulfillment, less stress and busyness. But it will require your trust that it will all work out even if you can't see the big picture right now.

2. The bigger the problem, the bigger the opportunity for improvement.

Major change means major opportunity. A fundamental change is your opportunity to incorporate the things you've been daydreaming about into your lifestyle. As long as you're going to make a change, why not go for what you really want? If you don't get it, you might end up getting close. Take out your journal and make a list of the biggest problems or challenges you face because of the busyness in your life. Next to each, note a drastic change you *could* make that would eliminate the problem. It doesn't matter if you don't think you would ever actually make the change, just write down everything that occurs to you. Often the best ideas come from this sort of brainstorming. And it helps when you can see that you have options. You may not choose many of the options for your life, but you do have a choice. You are stuck only if you choose to be stuck. You are now on a journey toward change, and the best way to make good choices is to consider all of your options. A hybrid of two or three almost-good options can often create the perfect solution.

3. Know your vision.

On Day 2, I asked you to create a vision of your ideal life. Consider that vision. Reread it. Doing so will give you clarity about the fundamental change you may need to make in your life in order to get to your vision. In fact, it may be very obvious, but without looking at the vision, you might miss it! Your vision is the next destination on your journey. For example, if your vision is more time for family and fun, you may determine that climbing the professional ladder is no longer a big priority for you. That might be your fundamental change—to simply do work you enjoy without the pressure of striving to run the company. This change in mind-set will empower you to achieve your vision. It is a shift in values that means giving up something you previously placed a high value on in order to get something else (family time and fun) on which you now place a higher value.

4. Change can happen suddenly. Jump on board.

The house I live in now was not even in my realm of thinking three months before we moved in. We were planning to move into a new development on the Potomac River in two years, after construction was complete. It would meet many of our wants—good location, on the water, close to the city. But after spending several weekends boating in Annapolis, Maryland, that year, we fell deeply in love with a town we already knew we really liked. Within a short time my husband was checking out homes and casually asking on Sunday afternoons, "Hey, you want to go look at some houses today?" "Sure, why not?" I'd respond. It never hurts to look, right? Within a few weeks we stumbled upon a house we loved and bought it. Suddenly our lives changed in a big way. What we didn't immediately realize is how much this move would improve our quality of life. The house serves our lifestyle, giving us space in the right places to do what we need and want to do on an everyday basis. Everyday errands are easier to handle because everything is so close. Much of what we need is in walking distance. Nothing is more than five miles away—and most of what we enjoy is within a two-mile radius. This change happened very quickly. Sometimes you must simply go with the flow when you explore opportunities to make a fundamental change in your life.

5. Remember that risk is reducible.
A drastic change doesn't need to be a hasty change. It is typically the risks of change—the "what ifs"—that generate the most fear. Make a list of the risks that concern you. Then ask, "How could I reduce my risk in each of these areas?"

6. Face forward.
Remember that the future is ahead of you, not behind you. Those whose eyes are looking back cannot see the opportunities that lie at their feet.

7. Expect fear. It's part of the process.
Don't let fear keep you on the verge of transition. When your intuition tells you it's time to make a move, *move!* Countless opportunities are lost because people waited too long to step out on faith.

MY CHALLENGE TO YOU TODAY

Open your mind to your possibilities. Is it time for you to move? Get a new job? Leave the workforce to become a stay-at-home parent?

Five-Minute Journal

If you were to do something that would really give you the opportunity to shift out of overdrive and take control of your time, what would it be? No little ideas here. Think BIG.

One-Minute Meditation

The power of choice lies within me. It is up to me to make decisions that create the space for a harmonious life to emerge.

DAY 14

Address Your
Adrenaline
Addiction

I get a lot done. People often ask me how I do it. My
frustration is that even though I get a lot done, I often feel empty when I reach a goal. And I immediately set out to reach a new one.
—DELIA, 29

One summer afternoon in the late 1990s, my close friend Jackie
came into my office to help with a couple of projects. Jackie was
off for the summer. Knowing that I had a lot on my plate with
an upcoming event, she offered to come in to help out. She had
been in the office for a couple of hours when I began to feel like
I was rushing her. Her pace was unhurried, yet each task was approached deliberately. My pace, while intentional, was fast. I
had never noticed how hurriedly I did everything. In fact, I
could be downright impatient with people who didn't move as
quickly as I. Jackie's unhurried pace wasn't calculated, and nei-
ther was mine. It was as though we each had a different natural
rhythm for going about our work. This rhythm can impact your
relationships and your work style.

Tune In to Your Natural Rhythm

In the years since, I have noticed this to be universally true. We each have a rhythm—a pace—at which we are most at ease and productive in life. Think of it as a personal speed limit. Like the minimum and maximum speed limits posted on an interstate, most people fall within a given range. Of course, even if your natural rhythm is on the high end of this range, it's quite possible you are pushing the speed limit, perhaps exceeding it. When you break your own personal speed limit, you'll notice yourself making mistakes, forgetting things, losing your keys, and so forth. Where do you think you fall on the spectrum? Are you within reasonable limits or speeding excessively—perhaps even waiting to the last minute to address issues, then using adrenaline to get things done?

There is a difference between being busy and being in a hurry. Being busy is about how much activity is in your life. Being in a hurry—or in overdrive—is about how fast you go about engaging in those activities. Today, I want you to notice how the two intersect in your life. Having a lot to do does not necessitate rushing. There are those who have a lot on their plates but never are in a hurry to get it all done. Perhaps you've encountered some of them and found yourself frustrated while waiting on them to do something for you. They get to it when they get to it, and it doesn't bother them one bit if that means others have to sit still and wait. Their motto is, "I'll get to it when I get to it."

Then there are people who, even when they are not particularly productive, live life at a fast pace. They are hasty in their decision making and rush through life trying to experience as much as possible as quickly as possible. These are the people who walk fast when there is nowhere in particular they need to be. They talk fast when there is plenty of time to talk. They eat fast by habit. They drive fast, even though they're not running late. They rush their kids; "Come on! Hurry up!" are four common words their kids have become used to hearing. There is a degree of urgency to everything in their lives, perhaps encouraged by the pace of culture and the world around them. Or perhaps encouraged by some inner issues that have convinced them that they are going to miss out on something, that they are behind and in a race to get or stay ahead.

Perhaps you know others who rush unnecessarily, but you feel adamantly that you rush out of necessity. There is so much packed into each day that the only way to get it all done is to do everything as quickly as possible. When you combine a full schedule with a habit of hurrying, the problem becomes overdrive.

Stop Breaking Your Own Speed Limit

There are days when you must move quickly if you are going to accomplish the tasks and activities you have for that day. Still, there is a point at which your speediness crosses the line to clumsiness. When that happens, the ensuing mistakes will cost you far more time than simply slowing your pace a bit. Like my fiasco at the airport that I mentioned on Day 3, you may have experienced this phenomenon in your life. When you find yourself moving so fast that you are likely to miss important information or make mistakes, then you know you are breaking your own personal speed limit and it's time to slow down. Begin noticing how quickly you do a variety of things in your life. Do you do any of the following?

- *Walk fast*
- *Talk fast*

- *Eat fast*
- *Drive fast*
- *Work fast*
- *Write fast*
- *____ fast*

I know I'm in a hurry when I can no longer read my own writing. I scribble on a sticky note and later struggle to read it. Have you ever had that happen? These are practical ways to notice when it's time to slow down. We'll talk more later on about discovering and tuning in to your natural rhythm so that you can find a pace that is optimal for your productivity and fulfillment.

Do You Have an Adrenaline Habit?

A few years ago my doctor warned me very sternly about my overdrive lifestyle. I had begun to forget things, my neck was in constant pain, and I was having digestive problems. The subject came up during a routine physical exam. When my physician pressed down gently on the area just below my sternum, I winced.

"That hurt?" he asked, surprised.

"Yes," I said, confused that he looked surprised.

"There's no reason that should hurt," he said, concerned. He then began asking a series of questions about my work and lifestyle.

"When you are on the computer, how many programs do you have open at any given time?" he asked. It seemed an odd question for diagnosis of a health problem, but I answered.

"Hmm. Depending on what I am working on, I may have four or five windows open at a time," I replied.

"Why?" he asked.

"Because I'm working on multiple documents and I go back and forth between the Internet and whatever projects I am working on," I explained.

"When you drive, do you do other things?" he asked.

"Well, yes," I admitted.

"Like what?" he probed.

"Usually I talk on the phone," I said. "Occasionally, if I'm in a big hurry, I eat. Why do you ask?"

The doctor went on to explain that it appeared I had been consistently operating on adrenaline, so much so that the adrenaline had begun to damage the lining of my esophagus. He ordered me to slow down, drop some of my activities, and be intentional about doing one thing at a time. For starters, he said, "Try driving without doing anything else but concentrating on driving."

"What if I have a headset? Can I talk on the phone?" I asked. It sounded reasonable enough, but he frowned, raised an eyebrow and said sternly, "Try doing nothing but driving."

Although a simple request, it was difficult to do. The temptation was always there to multitask. It felt like it was wasting time to drive without talking on the phone.

It didn't seem that serious of an issue to me—until I asked him what would happen if I did not change my lifestyle. "If you continue on this path, it could lead to ulcers, or eventually, stomach cancer," he told me. Stomach cancer? I thought, shocked. He had my attention. And my journey toward finding a way to be productive yet healthy, happy, and energetic began. The symptoms brought on by my adrenaline problem had plagued me for a couple of years, but I'd not paid them much attention. Now I take notice.

In fact, psychologists and doctors have pinpointed a problem that they deem "adrenaline addiction." Adrenaline increases your heart rate and raises your blood pressure. It also diverts blood away from the nonessential areas of your brain and internal organs and into your muscles. This is why adrenaline can increase speed and strength. It also decreases how much you feel pain.

The premise of adrenaline addiction is that some people, usually under the label "stress," use their own adrenaline as a drug. By creating intensity, they are able to repress the conscious emergence of particularly painful, underlying feelings of loss, disconnection, abandonment, or other issues. Adrenaline addiction, which can manifest itself in workaholism, is sometimes called the "respectable addiction." Since it manifests itself in productivity and results, it can be easily masked as hard work. But adrenaline is a natural chemical produced in the body as a response to stress that can give the body a feeling of a natural high. Here are some signs of adrenaline addiction:

- *The more pressure you are under, the better you perform.*

- *Checking items off of your to-do list excites you and makes you feel like you are really accomplishing something.*

- *You feel guilty about taking breaks in the middle of the day, let alone a vacation.*

- *You feel anxious when you do not have your cell phone, Internet connection, or text message device. You need to be in constant contact with people.*

- *You procrastinate until the last possible start time that will allow you to meet your deadline. You are driven by deadlines.*

- *If you weren't so busy, you'd have time to exercise.*

- *If you weren't so busy, you'd have more time to get together with people.*

- *You are spent and exhausted at the end of the day.*

- *You're not content unless there is some excitement in your life.*
- *Your friends and family just have to understand, your work is demanding and doesn't leave a lot of time for socializing.*
- *You need to be doing something all of the time.*
- *You are restless on uneventful vacations. It is uncomfortable to sit around doing nothing.*
- *You eat on the run—often in the car, at your desk, or standing up at the kitchen counter.*

Do any of the descriptions above look familiar to you? In the next chapter we'll discuss some specific ways to identify and overcome your adrenaline habit and get to the source of your overdrive tendency.

MY CHALLENGE TO YOU TODAY
Carve out a period today to do absolutely nothing. It might be just twenty minutes. It might be a few hours. Sit or lie somewhere comfortable and pleasant, and just be.

FIVE-MINUTE JOURNAL
Do you have a habit of using adrenaline to get things done? When do you tend to use adrenaline? What do you want to do instead?

ONE-MINUTE MEDITATION
I am peaceful and relaxed, yet productive.

DAY : 15

Create Deliberate
Daily Rituals

> When I get up with enough time to sit in my
> kitchen, have a cup of coffee, and read the paper be-
> fore starting my day, the whole day seems to be more
> productive.
>
> —JOHNNY, 48

Now that the weather is warm and the sun rises before
6:00 A.M., I am enjoying the ritual of an early-morning walk. In
fact, I have a list of seven things that empower me to start my
day off in a joyful, effective way posted just inside my closet,
where I can be reminded of them. They include rituals such as
thirty minutes of exercise, listening to good music, quiet time,
and eating breakfast. When I created my set of rituals, I wasn't
sure I had time for all of them. Now I feel like I don't have time
not to do each and every one.

How you begin your morning largely determines the flow of
your entire day. Is your morning a frantic sprint for the door? Or
a well-thought-out series of actions that prepare you to have a
joyful, productive day?

Often the small, simple changes you make in your schedule
can create a sense of greater control and satisfaction. Your

habits create your future. Today, I challenge you to be deliberate about how you start your day. What daily habits would you like to enjoy in your life? Make a list of five things that would enrich your day. For the next seven days, incorporate those habits into your life and see how it goes. You can do anything for seven days, right? If it makes a positive difference for you, keep doing it.

Here are five simple ideas to help you create deliberate, daily habits:

1. Write a vision of your ideal morning.

What are the things you would like to be able to do and enjoy as you begin your day? Make a simple list. Then post it in places—such as on the refrigerator door, inside the medicine cabinet, or next to your alarm clock—where you will be reminded of your ideal morning.

2. Estimate how much time each morning ritual will take you.

You will find that if you think this through ahead of time, you can design a morning that energizes you for the rest of your day. Choose things that you can do now without a tremendous amount of effort. For example, if you haven't been working out at all, and you insist that your morning ritual will include an hour workout at the gym, it's likely your ritual will not last. Make your morning rituals and habits easy.

3. Identify a simple way to connect with loved ones in the mornings.

It can be as simple as a kiss when you wake up or being sure to hug your children when they get up. Mornings offer the opportunity to connect with your children, spouse, or other loved ones who live in the household. Sit down for breakfast together for ten minutes. Remember my client Susan, whom I mentioned on Day 9? She started a ten-minutes-in-the-morning ritual of having breakfast with her young son to help ease her concern that she was not spending enough quality time with him. Perhaps you connect over a cup of a coffee or orange juice, or by exercising together, or with some other ritual. Find something easy and enjoyable.

4. Choose things you truly want to do, not what you "should" do.

The habits that you choose should be ones that will help you better express your values and who you are. Do not choose habits that you think you should do or that others think you should do, but the ones that will truly nourish you and help you create the kind of life you believe is possible. This is all about upgrading your everyday quality of life.

5. Test your habits—and adjust them.

Commit to practicing your habits for the next seven days. Notice what works and does not work. Personal growth happens when we take action and then learn from our actions, tweaking and improving them along the way. For now, just try your habits for seven days and notice how it impacts your entire week.

Seize the Day, Then End the Day

How you begin your day has a tremendous impact on your productivity. How you end your day can have an impact on your emotions as well as your readiness for the following morning. When you end your day haphazardly—for example, falling asleep on the sofa or working so late that you end up going to bed too late and feeling groggy in the morning—you sabotage your success. I have always loved this quote from Ralph Waldo Emerson:

> Finish each day and be done with it. You have done what you could. Some blunders and absurdities have crept in; forget them as soon as you can. Tomorrow is a new day; you shall begin it serenely and with too high a spirit to be encumbered with your old nonsense.

The quote serves as a reminder of the importance of putting boundaries around our time and expectations of each new day. Today, I would like to simply remind you to "finish each day and be done with it." Forgive yourself for not accomplishing everything you "could" have. Relax and be at peace with simply doing what you were able. Give yourself permission to make a few mistakes, be imperfect, and inadvertently get off track from time to time. After all, you are human. One of my friends—a successful executive and single mom of three—told me a few years ago that she had learned that "being superwoman is a super myth." She was right on point. You can get into the habit of taking on too much responsibility and then expecting yourself to handle every responsibility perfectly and expediently. Before long you can become exhausted and even burned out.

Here are a few ways to practice "finishing each day and being done with it":

1. Leave your work at work.
If you work from home, do the same. When your workday ends, mentally shift from professional life mode to personal life mode. This is a chance to practice discipline because that is exactly what it takes to "leave your work at work" when you are succeeding in your work. The key to remember is that you are pur-

suing a self-care lifestyle—one that does not give work a higher spot on your list of priorities than your personal life.

2. Let your to-do's spill over into the next day.
As we will discuss on Day 16, to-do lists are often quite unrealistic. Be honest with yourself about what you can actually accomplish in a day. If something doesn't get completed, move it to another day. Put your to-do's into proper perspective. Sometimes we stress out over tasks that are not urgent matters. If there is not enough time or energy for you to accomplish your to-do, let it go. There is nothing you can do about time lost. Forgive yourself if you feel you wasted time during the day. Beating yourself up won't solve the dilemma. Instead, acknowledge your mistake and make a decision to do better tomorrow.

3. Every conflict does not have to be resolved today.
If you've had a tough day with coworkers, your children, a spouse, or a friend, don't feel pressured to always resolve the issue the same day. I'm not suggesting that you should avoid difficult conversations, but rather that it is important to identify the right time and place to have them. Sometimes waiting a day or two can allow heated emotions to cool and a more productive conversation to occur. Be intentional about what you allow to distract you from your priorities on any given day. Emotional conflicts can often steer you off track, leaving you frustrated at the end of the day, when the conflict is still unresolved and your work still undone. So learn to distinguish between urgent conflicts that need to be addressed immediately and conflicts that do not have to be addressed in the moment. A conflict needs to be addressed immediately if the consequences of putting it off until tomorrow have ramifications that undermine your priorities, values, or vision. If the only window of opportunity to address it occurs today, and it is significant enough for you to take

time away from another priority, then by all means address it. I am not suggesting you avoid conflict, only that you do not allow it to become a stumbling block to seizing the moments in your day.

4. Clear your mind to focus on the present.

When you find yourself focused on all that you did not accomplish during the day, take a deep breath and make a decision to focus on your goal again tomorrow. Refuse to mull over moments that have passed earlier in your day that you will never get back. Instead, maximize the moment you are in right now by enjoying it fully. It, too, will never be regained. This is a lesson in self-care in that this process gives you permission to be human.

Often when talking with clients or even audience members during a speaking engagement, it amazes me how often people speak of their disorganization, procrastination, or difficulty in handling an overloaded schedule as though it is unique to their situation. To some degree, most people struggle with overestimating how much they can accomplish in a day. Many people say they will get started on something, but get distracted or drag their feet. You are not alone.

I am not saying you will be happy about it, but if you have the expectation that your day will not always unfold the way you think it should, it becomes easier to accept the fact at the end of the day that you didn't do all that you set out to do. You set yourself up for disappointment when you expect more from yourself than you are able to give. Don't live in the past by rehashing what you "should" have done. Don't live in the future by setting an expectation you can't live up to tomorrow. Instead, at the end of your day, shift gently into the present moment and allow yourself to relax and appreciate yourself, whatever great or small feats you have accomplished.

5. End your day on purpose.

Do you sometimes fall asleep while watching TV? Do you drift off to sleep vowing to read one more chapter in a book only to wake up with the lights on and an open book on your pillow? Studies show that most people have a more restful night's sleep when they have a bedtime routine consisting of dimmed lights and low or no noise in the hour before going to sleep—followed by turning off the lights and resting until drifting off to sleep. For some, this takes practice. If you are used to haphazardly ending your day, it can feel strange to have such a routine. But just as I asked you to create deliberate morning rituals, I invite you to also create deliberate evening rituals. A bath, a cup of chamomile tea (helps calm you), a good book (although boring books can help you fall asleep, too), soft music—all of these can become your evening rituals. End your day intentionally and you will find yourself energized to take on tomorrow.

By bookending your day with deliberate morning and evening rituals—and seizing the moments in the midday—you will feel a greater sense of control over your time. These rituals are simple and do not take much time. It is the act of being intentional about how you live day to day that is most empowering. On your journey from busyness to self-care and fruitfulness, this level of intention is a powerful companion.

My Challenge to You Today

Create a vision for your ideal morning. Identify the three to five rituals you would like to incorporate into the start of your day and practice them for the next seven days.

Five-Minute Journal

What will you have to change in order to create your ideal morning? Are you willing to make those changes? Are you ending your day well? What shift could you make to "seize the day, then end the day"?

One-Minute Meditation

Seize the day, then end the day.

DAY : 16

Tame Your To-Do List

I have different to-do lists for work and personal
stuff. I get a lot done, but the list never seems to get
any shorter.

—MARIA, 42

Have you ever been overwhelmed by the series of projects or errands waiting to be checked off of your to-do list? If you are not
careful, it can be easy to focus more on what you have not done
than on what you have done. When one of my clients began
coaching, she always wanted to end the session by reviewing
what was being added to her to-do list that week. At first I
didn't think much of it. She is very organized and action-
oriented, so it seemed like a tactic that worked well for her. But
as we continued our conversations, it became obvious that her
to-do list was more of a hindrance than a help.

She was so focused on what she needed to do to achieve her
goals that she never reflected on who she needed to become in
order to reach them. One of the primary qualities she needed to
develop was trust. She admitted that she always tried to control
everything in her life, but wanted to learn to trust that if she followed her path, everything would unfold as it should. Instead,

she was busy trying to anticipate what was coming two or three steps ahead so that she could be ready. It was exhausting. Her to-do list was two pages long. As soon as she would cross something off, something else would be added. Perhaps yours isn't completely out of control, but it may still be a bit unruly—giving you the feeling that you just aren't getting enough done. To be clear, I think to-do lists can be very helpful. I have an informal to-do list that I write on a printed version of my weekly calendar. As the days go by, I am able to see how much progress I am making as the week moves forward. To-do lists give you an organized outlet for staying on track and productive with your goals and activities throughout a given week. Yes, it can be stressful to attempt to remember everything you have to do, so don't keep it all in your head. But I have some rules that keep it from getting out of hand:

1. Limit your to-do list to simple tasks.

Since half of most people's to-do list is never completed anyway, why not limit your to-do's to simple things you don't want to forget rather than major goals or projects? A to-do list item such as "Pick up prescription" is a simple task. "Write business plan," on the other hand, is a major goal. The weight of a major goal on your to-do list can make you anxious and keep you from feeling a sense of accomplishment at the end of each day. Instead, divide a major goal into bite-size tasks for your to-do list. It is particularly noteworthy that those who struggle most with procrastination often have major projects listed as to-do's. Because the task is overwhelming, with no specific action step attached to it, they never even get started.

2. Make your to-do list optional.

If you are attached to your to-do list, give yourself a break for one week. Try operating without a list. You might be surprised by just how productive you are. By focusing on your present moments—rather than on what you should have done yesterday and what must be done by tomorrow—you can get more done. When there is space in your life, it is easier to accomplish this successfully. It requires being in a state of flow, where you instinctively know what to do next and you just do it. There's nothing holding you back and no distractions vying for your attention.

3. Do something for yourself.

If you decide to use a to-do list, make sure it includes things "to do" for yourself as well. Ask yourself, "How would I like to pamper myself?" Then schedule it on your calendar. Schedule in fun, exercise, and rest periods as well, weighing those as significantly on your list of to-do's as the responsibilities that are for the benefit of others. Taking this approach to your to-do list also gives it some lightness, balancing it so that it is not just task-oriented.

4. Acknowledge your progress.

At the end of each day, make a "progress" list. It is easy to focus on what you haven't done, but each day, acknowledge what you have done, pat yourself on the back, and look forward to tomorrow. Your progress list can be written or kept as a mental note. Crossing items off of a list can be gratifying, but it is equally rewarding to view your accomplishments not as just things to cross off but as progress toward a greater goal.

5. Be realistic.

Don't put so much on your to-do list that checking it off will be impossible. This is a sure way to constantly feel as though you are playing catch-up. Set yourself up for success—not failure—by writing a list that is doable within the time you have available. Be realistic by recognizing the difference between a real deadline and a self-imposed one. You can exhaust yourself trying to meet every deadline—from those with small consequences (like getting your rental video back to the store on time) to those with potentially major consequences (like filing your taxes on time). Learn to distinguish the ones that will have a true impact from the ones that are flexible. And be willing to be flexible with the deadlines you set for yourself. When it comes to deadlines, ask yourself, "What impact will this have on me a year from now?" Under suggestion #1, I recommended that the tasks on your list be simple. I also recommend that they be achievable within the time frame of your list. Specify the period for which you are writing the list. For example, you may have a list for a day or one for the entire week. If there is no way you can accomplish a particular task in the time frame of your list, don't put it on there. An easy way to do this is to note the approximate amount of time each task will take next to each item on the list. At the bottom of the list, tally up the total time it will require. If there are more to-do's than you have time for, make adjustments. Move some items to another day or week, or delegate some items. Or you can do what I suggest next—be brave and cut them from the list!

6. Cross a few things off the list altogether.
Everything does not need to get done, or at least doesn't need to get done *today*. Sometimes you simply need to drop a thing or two to keep your sanity and enjoy your life. Make peace with the fact that there will always be more to do, but that doesn't mean you should spend every waking moment trying to do it. It's also important to cross those items off of your list that are unnecessary. Don't create more work for yourself than you have to. For example, you may insist on running some errands in person that could be done more efficiently online—such as grocery shopping and banking. Notice what "busywork" you've created on

your schedule. Cut out all of it! The more time you spend doing unnecessary activities, the less time you have for yourself and your priorities.

7. Align your actions with your priorities.

Does your to-do list reflect the things you say matter most in your life? Rank your five most important priorities. Consider how you have spent your time over the last week. Do your priorities and actions line up? The way you spend your time is the best indicator of how you live your life, and your to-do list should emanate from these priorities. So before you begin writing your list, look back at your vision and your goals from Day 1. Then create your list from it. For many people there is a disconnection between their day-to-day to-do's versus what they say is important to them. You can change this easily by following the simple to-do list format below or creating one of your own.

The Realistic To-Do List

Your realistic to-do list should contain several simple elements, including your vision, your top three goals for the month, the dates or period covered on the list, the list itself, and how much time each item on the list will take. Below is a realistic sample to-do list; you can create and print one of your own. The "vision" should be a synopsis of the vision or model you created on Day 1. It will serve as a consistent reminder of the lifestyle you are committed to create for yourself. In the Top Three Goals section, jot down your primary goals for the month. Your goals represent specific objectives for your life that will lead you to the vision. You can later create an electronic version, then type in today's date or "the week of" and the dates for the list.

My To-Do List

Vision:

....

Top three goals for the month

....

....

....

Period: How much time
To-Do's   will this take?

....

....

....

Total time:

....

My Challenge to You Today

Tame your to-do list. Take a look at what you have to do and eliminate something nonurgent from the list.

Five-Minute Journal

In what ways are your actions currently out of alignment with the priorities you stated in your vision on Day 1? In what way could you readjust your actions to truly reflect your vision and what matters most to you?

One-Minute Meditation

My to-do list is an optional, flexible tool that represents my true priorities.

DAY : **17**

Set Your Personal Priority Criteria

> I know what I say my priorities are, it's getting to
> them every day that's the struggle!
> —MIRIAM, 35

You can easily discern your true priorities by how you actually spend time on a day-to-day basis. Whatever is getting your time is your true priority right now. If your time is being spent on activities that are not a priority, it's time for a change. One of the best ways to determine what activities to keep and which ones to drop is to make sure they each meet your personal priority test. A personal priority test is a set of criteria or standards you set for what deserves your time. So just how do you set criteria that enable you to make decisions about opportunities and requests?

First, declare your priorities. List them in order of importance. For example, your list may look something like this:

Spiritual Life

Marriage and Family

Health and Self-Care

Friendships and Community
Work
Finances

Then, consider the criteria you want to set for what gets your time. Start with the list below and add to it if necessary. As you think about all of your existing commitments and activities, and entertain new requests or projects, ask yourself how many of the following statements are true for the activity in question. The more of these you are able to answer, the more compatible the activity for your schedule:

- *It fulfills my purpose.*
- *It will be good for my relationship with my spouse.*
- *It is good for me.*
- *It enriches my relationships with family or friends.*
- *It gives me an opportunity to create more space in my life.*
- *It gives me energy, confidence, or some other valuable benefit that empowers me to make progress toward my vision.*
- *It moves me closer to my vision.*
- *Other* ....
- *Other* ....

It is also important to play devil's advocate and identify the deal breakers for any request. If one of the following statements holds true for a request or commitment you are struggling with, then you know to say "no" to the opportunity. These are disqualifiers:

- *It drains my energy.*
- *I do not feel at peace about it.*

- *It is detrimental to my most important relationships.*
- *It is counter to my values.*
- *I do not have time to do it or I will have to give up a more important priority in order to make room.*
- *It is a poor financial decision.*
- *It is detrimental to my health and well-being.*
- *Other* ....
- *Other* ....

The goal is to engage in opportunities that meet as many of your criteria as possible while meeting none of your disqualifiers. If there is something you feel inclined to add to your plate, yet it does not make it through your personal priority test successfully, explore ways to adjust the activity so that it will meet your criteria. Be creative. Investigate your options. *Negotiate.*

The Reward of Negotiating for What You Want

Diana was frustrated with her work situation. It was out of control, and stress-related health problems had begun to plague her. She needed to do something different. Her company had essentially given her the jobs of three people, and dutifully, she had juggled the impossible workload successfully. Now her contract was up for renewal and she felt inclined to ask for a raise.

"Is that all you're going to request of them?" I asked.

"What do you mean?" she replied.

"Well, you've made it clear that you have too much on your plate. An increase in pay is not going to solve that. What do you *really* want from them?"

"That's easy," she responded. "I want to love my work again, and that would mean not having to do so much of it! It's taken the joy out of my job. And they would pay me quite a bit more—and they would give me more time to do the projects for which I am responsible."

"Is it perhaps time for you to ask for all three of those things?"

She thought for a moment. "Hmmph. It would feel good to ask for it. Lord knows I work hard enough." She knew she would shortchange herself if she asked for only money. And she was kidding herself if she believed it would be enough to satisfy her goal of decreasing her stress level to prevent further health problems. She needed to get off of the endless treadmill she ran on each day.

"So, will you ask for all of what you want?" I probed.

She replied, apprehensive yet excited, "Yes, I will. The worst thing that could happen is they'd say 'no' and I wouldn't get the contract again. And at this point, I'm so worn out that I think they'd do me a favor not to continue our agreement."

Diana met with the company leaders and stated her wishes—a contract to do half as much work, with more time to do it, and a ten-thousand-dollar increase in fees. The management team had a meeting about it. She held her breath and waited for the response. To her delight, they met every one of her requests!

When you have no criteria or boundaries, others will put as much on you as you will take—and they will give you as little reward for your efforts as possible. When you stand up for yourself, adjustments will happen. Be willing to accept consequences and not change your criteria. This is why you have criteria—criteria by which you live, love, and work. Your criteria reminds you of your vision and all that you stand for.

Saying "No" to Some Things

Yesterday I received a request to review a manuscript and endorse a book. It was from someone I know only vaguely. Why is it difficult to say "no"? It was the fifth request in six weeks. It is an honor to have so many requests, but since I was in the middle of writing my own book, common sense told me I would simply have to muster up the courage to decline. The problem is, common sense does not always prevail when it comes to your schedule. Saying no causes such anxiety for so many people. But what is that anxiety really about?

When I searched for my answer to that question, the only thought that came to mind is my concern about what others would think of me for saying "no." "Hmmph. She's obviously not as nice as she appears to be. I thought her mission was about helping people, and here I ask for help, and she's too busy to give it." Recognizing the fear as it appeared, I graciously declined—and felt grateful to have enough worthwhile opportunities in my life that I must say "no" to some of them. I haven't always felt this way, which is why I am able to easily discuss the issues that arise from being overloaded and overdriven. It used to pain me to say no, even to requests I had no desire to do. I just didn't like having to say no. People pleasing is another fear-based behavior that contributes to the busyness lifestyle.

Often we need to dig beneath the surface of our fears. Is it about being too busy, or is it about priorities? Perhaps it is a combination of both. At certain points in your life you must realize that in order to succeed, you will need to make some tough choices. That means setting boundaries around your time, which ultimately means saying no to some requests and opportunities. It means not making exceptions every time you are asked to do something that falls outside of your boundaries. It means being comfortable enough with who you are and how many hours you have in the day to admit when you simply do not have the time to meet the demands of everyone who asks.

Nor should you feel pressured to respond to requests immediately. When someone makes a request, you don't need to give them an immediate answer. "Let me think about that and get back to you," or "I'll let you know tomorrow (or next week, etc.)" will suffice. Especially for those who are people pleasers, it is critical that you don't answer "yes" on the spot. You will often end up regretting your commitment later.

The act of saying no does not have to be difficult. You don't have to make up excuses, you simply need to speak your truth. It feels good to be clear about your needs, abilities, and limitations—and to honor them. Even if people don't like hearing "no" from you, they must respect your ability to be honest with them and true to yourself. If you agree with all that I am saying here, but still have doubts about some of the things you need to say no to, use these questions as a coaching tool to help you determine how to say no to a request:

- Why don't I want to say yes to the request?

....

- What will I have to say no to, if I say yes to the request? (Remember, "downtime," "sleep," and "rest" are legitimate to-do's for you.)

....

- What am I afraid will happen if I say no?

....

- Is that likely to happen? ....

- What would be the consequences of that happening?

....

- Am I willing to pay those consequences?

....

- Am I willing to take my chances and say no anyway?

....

If you are unwilling to pay the consequences or take your chances that your fear will come true, then say yes to the request. If you realize that your fear is irrational, unlikely to happen, and that you are willing to pay the potential consequences, then it's time to articulate how you will say no. Look again to your answer under, "Why don't I want to say yes to the request?" This is your truth. In a thoughtful way, state this truth to whomever has made the request. In some instances you may choose to reword it, but do not lose the essence of your message or give in to any temptation to lie. Just say what you need to say and move on. They'll be okay.

My Challenge to You Today

Set your personal priority criteria and practice sticking to them.

Five-Minute Journal

What criteria will I measure opportunities/requests by in order to determine what goes on my calendar?

One-Minute Meditation

When I feel stressed by all that I have to do, I remember that it doesn't all have to get done *today*.

DAY 18

Take Time to Gain Perspective

> Every time I accomplish something important to me, it's like I'm waiting for the fireworks to go off at the finish line, but they never do. It's just like, okay, that's done . . . now on to the next thing.
>
> —TANYA, 25

I just stepped in from the balcony of my hotel room on Miami Beach. A few quiet moments gazing at the gorgeous ocean coastline and a couple of days in an environment outside of my norm always opens my mind to new ideas, options, and dreams. Have you ever noticed how getting away gives you a new perspective on things? Today, I challenge you to consider ways—big and small—that you can put yourself in a different environment purely for the sake of renewing your mind. Breaking away from your regular routine can provide the inner renewal and energy you need to make decisions, persevere through challenges, and resist getting drawn into the drama and issues that can tempt you daily.

Throughout my life I have often found water to be a haven of peace, rest, and reflection. As a child in Florida, the Gulf of Mexico was my backyard—literally. We lived on an Air Force base and our house sat just two hundred feet from the water's edge. As I swung back and forth on my swing or played in my sandbox, I would watch dolphins jump out of the water. But even when I lived in Denver and Dallas, I gravitated toward lakes and reservoirs on sunny days. What environment creates a sense of peace and relaxation for you? How could you carve out more time to spend there?

I want to encourage you to find a place that allows you to forget the hectic pace of life—even if for only a few moments—and enjoy that place regularly. Having an environment that nourishes you is essential to replenishing your energy. Just as important, a nurturing environment often helps you clarify your thoughts and deepen your ability to connect spiritually and with yourself. In that space, decisions become clearer and relaxation is easier.

Major epiphanies in my life have occurred while out of my normal environment. My epiphany about my life purpose came while on a trip to Seattle, Washington, in 1999. As I already told you, an inkling that I would be leaving Dallas in one year to live near the water occurred one afternoon while spending time at a local park near a lake in Dallas in 2002. Sometimes the inklings and attitude shifts that occur from putting yourself in a different environment can give you a better perspective on a frustrating situation at work or at home, defuse your stress at the end of a rough day, or simply renew your mind in the midst of multitasking. I'd like to share four ideas for getting away that may be just what you need to renew your mind:

1. Do something different.
It's so easy to get caught in the same routines day after day, weekend after weekend, and year after year. Identify new places where you'd like to eat, visit, relax, or have fun. This week,

commit to shaking up your normal routine with something different that will stimulate and nourish your mind.

2. Go away for the weekend.
A weekend getaway is like a miniature vacation. It is something you can do even if you don't have the chance right now to go away for a week or two. And it is a great way to refresh your spirit between vacations.

3. Take advantage of beauty in your own backyard.
It amazes me how often many of us take for granted the nature that is all around us. Having lived in some beautiful places—Florida, Germany, Colorado, and California—I didn't recognize how much I'd taken my scenic locales for granted until I moved to a place that didn't have a beach or mountains. While in Dallas, I learned to appreciate that beauty doesn't have to be grand in order to nurture our spirits. Get out and take a walk. Go to the park. Enjoy trees rustling in the breeze, birds chirping, and flowers blooming. And if you live in a particularly scenic area, by all means, take advantage of it!

4. Take a real vacation.
There is nothing like a true respite from the cares of everyday life. Don't shortchange yourself by calling a weekend a real vacation. Take out your calendar, block off a week or more, and write a vision of your ideal vacation. It might be an exotic trip—or it could be a peaceful period of nothingness right at home.

My Challenge to You Today

Take five minutes right now to ponder what you would like to do to "get away" and put yourself in a new environment. Then take action to make it happen.

Five-Minute Journal

In what ways would some time away help you gain perspective on your situation? What action would help you gain the perspective you need today?

One-Minute Meditation

I welcome a fresh perspective on my schedule.

DAY 19

Celebrate Your Milestones!

> It's the little wins along the way that keep me motivated to reach my vision.
>
> —COURTNEY, 29

One of my clients, Selene, moved into her new townhouse and found herself torn. It was a major accomplishment, buying her first home in a great part of town, but she had little time to celebrate because some exciting opportunities had fallen in her lap and she was busy trying to seize them for fear they might pass her by. She loved the house but complained, "I find myself pulled between work and a desire to sit in my new home and read a good book, take a nap, or walk around my neighborhood. And when I'm not fighting an urge to sit and relax or stroll around, then it is an urge to finish furniture shopping and decorating." At first she attributed it solely to procrastination. "Getting distracted is not hard to do when it's time to do something that requires focus and concentration," she admitted. But this distraction was different. The pull was very persistent. You know in your spirit when a feeling leaves you anxious and often there is a message in your feelings. She decided to stop fighting the urges and begin following them. It was a good move. "I learned that what I really wanted was to feel settled," she discovered. "I needed to create room in my life to acknowledge my transition and settle in."

It can be easy to make major changes in your life without slowing down to appreciate and settle in to your new state of being. Whether it is a move, a new job, a new relationship, or the end of an old one, notice the turning point as it is happening. Ask yourself, "What do I need right now in order to feel at peace?"

In an effort to accomplish more, we often don't take time to stop and celebrate what we have already done before moving on to the next goal. Imagine yourself running a marathon—and then discovering at the end that the finish line is the starting block for your next race. No time to bask in the glory of your hard work and perseverance, no time to celebrate, only time to do it all over again. It would be exhausting, disappointing, and unfulfilling. It makes your accomplishments anticlimactic when you cruise through them without acknowledging and celebrating what it took for you to get there. An important way to slow down and enjoy the journey is to celebrate your milestones along the way.

Your accomplishments don't have to be major to deserve acknowledgment. Only you know what it has taken for you to get to where you are. So for me, writing a book at a joyful pace and on time is definitely worthy of celebration! What milestone could you celebrate today? In case you're saying, "Valorie, I don't have anything to celebrate right now," consider these:

Making It to Day 19

No doubt, by this point on your journey through this book, you've made some progress. Even small changes deserve a pat on the back. You've made a decision to change your lifestyle and you are on a new path. It is worthy of acknowledgment!

The Growth and Maintenance of an Important Relationship

Whether it is a relationship with your spouse, significant other, family member, or a new friend, celebrate the existence of loving relationships in your life. Perhaps you met your best friend ten years ago this summer. Maybe you've forgiven someone after a long period of hurt or anger. Celebrate your achievement.

A Visible Manifestation of Your Spiritual Growth

Remember how you used to be short-tempered with people who cut you off in traffic? Now you slow down and let them in. Or perhaps you used to worry incessantly about the things happening in your life, and now you remain calm in even the most difficult situations. You have grown and expanded as a person. Celebrate this growth by noticing just how far you've come and being thankful for your progress.

You've Shifted to a Healthier Lifestyle

So your goal was to lose twenty-five pounds and you've lost ten? Congratulations! Especially for goals that are as measurable as weight loss, it is important to weigh the intangibles along with your weight. Celebrate the discipline you've exhibited in drinking more water, taking walks regularly, and giving up those potato chips. In the long run, your healthy habits will be more important than achieving a specific weight.

You Curbed Your Spending

Now, I'm not suggesting that you celebrate your improved financial habits by spending a lot of money for the celebration! Like engaging in healthier habits, improving your financial habits can be easily measured. When you pay off a credit card or a car, or reach a savings goal, celebrate the focus and discipline it took for you to accomplish such a milestone. Life is worthy of celebration. Don't hold your breath to celebrate only at the finish line of your goals. Celebrate the journey. As you grow in various areas of your life, pat yourself on the back. Notice how far you've come. It will fuel motivation to keep on growing.

My Challenge to You Today

Identify three milestones that will indicate to you that you are making good progress toward freeing your time, reclaiming your schedule, and reconnecting with what matters most. Name three ways you'd like to celebrate each milestone. Remember, celebration is about acknowledgment. So whether this will be a major celebration or a small one is not the point. This is about embracing the journey by giving yourself credit for the steps you've taken.

Five-Minute Journal

What could you celebrate right now about your progress? How would you like to go about doing that?

One-Minute Meditation

I choose to celebrate my progress regularly. My life is worthy of celebration.

DAY 20

Stop So You Can Catch Up

> Sometimes I just take a day off to run errands and
> catch up with stuff that's been on my to-do list too
> long.
>
> —MARIAN, 47

It was seemingly a weekday like the others that had been
whizzing by as I got used to my new life as a married person living halfway across the country from my home of eight years. The
previous few months had been a whirlwind, and I had not paid
much attention to how I was adjusting. I missed my mom and
brother, and the many friends I'd left back in Dallas. I was also
adjusting to a cultural change, having never previously lived on
the East Coast. I had to learn to navigate the highways and
streets of Maryland and the District of Columbia as well as
nearby Virginia, which was just a four-mile drive from home.
Wedding gifts were still in boxes in the living room, causing un-
wanted clutter and stress in our environment. But with nowhere
to put them, I was not particularly motivated to unpack them.
Every time I looked into the living room on the way to the
kitchen, I looked at the big pile.

On this particular day, my husband decided to work from home. My days had become a multitasking frenzy as I simultaneously worked, cooked, and did laundry. I had just dropped off a warm load of clothes in the bedroom when the timer went off on something I had in the oven, and I raced to the kitchen hoping to remove the baked chicken and get downstairs for a conference call that would start in two minutes. I must have looked frantic because he looked perplexed by the way I was running around. "Baby?" he asked, concerned and laughing at the same time. "Is this how you work every day?"

It's amazing how we can practice habits alone that look ridiculous when someone puts a mirror in front of us by questioning our methods. I soon realized that I had not given myself any transition time to adjust to my new home, my new life, and my new work environment. Instead, I forged ahead, starting to work immediately after moving. What I really needed to do was stop (by taking some time off, even if only for one week) so I could make a solid mental and physical transition, then begin work again.

When you encounter a transition in life, it is important to stop so that you can enter a new phase with an uncluttered mind, environment, or schedule. Whether it is a new job, new home, or new spouse, make it your rule to give yourself time between where you were and where you are headed in order to address the inevitable needs and potential challenges that arise from a transition. This concept is not only important for a transition, but also when you find yourself falling behind.

When your calendar is overloaded for an extended period of time, it is inevitable that you may begin missing deadlines, breaking promises, apologizing, and running late on a regular basis. In fact, it can even become a way of life. More than half of the respondents to the Busyness Survey stated that they consistently feel as though they are trying to "catch up." Here are a few of the ways to know that you need to stop so you can catch up:

- *You have projects and promises that are constantly nagging at you because you know they are overdue.*
- *You can't see more than half of the top of your desk because it's so cluttered.*
- *You don't have time to clean your house—or even time to call a maid service to clean it!*
- *You feel scattered, you're forgetting things, or missing deadlines.*
- *Things that you normally keep in order are becoming out of control.*

Today, I invite you to stop racing to get things done and actually get ahead for a change. It begins with creating an environment that supports your ability to get things done and energizes you to keep moving forward.

You need an environment that empowers you to think clearly and wade through all that comes your way so that you can focus on what really matters most. By scheduling time to catch up and get ahead, you'll find yourself being more relaxed and productive.

1. Get ahead once and for all.

If running behind has become a lifestyle for you, you can change it. But you must schedule some time to get ahead once and for all. Make a list of every area in which you are behind. Then identify specific elements that would empower you to get ahead and stay ahead. For example, if you regularly allow bills to fall through the cracks, schedule one day each month (or a day at the beginning and middle of the month) to pay them. This way, rather than trying to remember every due date, you will pay your bills on one or two days each month. If you routinely miss deadlines at work, schedule some time to get caught up and time to complete projects one to two weeks in advance. Then maintain your ahead-of-schedule routine so that the norm becomes being ahead of schedule rather than "on schedule."

2. Schedule one "catch up" day per week.
One of the keys to staying ahead is to schedule time to stay ahead. Set aside time one day each week to catch up with the loose ends that feel like they are about to unravel your entire schedule. Whether it's housework, finances, family time, or work, knowing that you have time in your schedule to "catch up" gives you the breathing room you need to keep the stress from piling on.

3. Promise little, if anything at all.
One of the best techniques for taking the pressure off of yourself is to "underpromise and overdeliver." If a client or boss asks for a project on a Monday, don't promise you'll deliver it by Wednesday even if you think you can. Instead, offer to have it by the following Monday. Then when you deliver on Wednesday, you look great. And if you can't get it done until Friday, you're still ahead of schedule! If you promise it by Wednesday and deliver on Friday, you didn't keep your word and the other person will be disappointed or aggravated. The same holds true when communicating with family, friends, or anyone else. Refuse to overobligate yourself.

4. Hire some help.
Who says you have to do everything yourself? From a maid service or babysitter to an accountant or personal trainer, consider hiring the help you need to get your life on track.

5. Lighten your load.

It's possible to create a schedule that is impossible to fulfill. A schedule that is too overloaded will keep you running behind indefinitely. Be willing to drop activities from your life that aren't serving your vision, your family, or your values. Trying to be "superwoman" or "superman" will only leave you exhausted, and even ill. Take care of yourself. You don't have to do everything!

My Challenge to You Today

Make a decision to get ahead and stay ahead. Schedule some time on your calendar to catch up.

Five-Minute Journal

What's the one area of my life in which I find myself consistently behind? What is the root cause of the problem? What could I do to catch up and stay ahead?

One-Minute Meditation

I can keep up with all of the responsibilities of my life with ease.

DAY 21

Finally Break Your Procrastination Habit

> I often procrastinate because if I'm not going to do it right, I'd rather not even bother to start. Unfortunately, that means stuff starts piling up— and at some point I've got to do it. By the time that time comes, I'm overwhelmed.
>
> —NATALIE, 39

Cara was swamped at work. A big project was due at work in three days, but she was frustrated because her car needed to be taken in for repairs. It was starting up sporadically and she'd gotten stuck on the way home the day before. Adding to the list of to-do's was a doctor's appointment for her teenage daughter the next day. She'd been lucky to get it scheduled at the last minute. Her daughter needed a physical by the end of the week as a requirement to participate in varsity track, and fortunately there had been a cancellation. Her husband was out of town on a business trip and wouldn't be able to help with either the car or the doctor's appointment. Cara wanted help on prioritizing and meeting her looming work deadline despite the personal matters demanding her attention. Her predicament was particularly curious because just three weeks earlier she'd talked happily about how much free time she'd been enjoying.

"It seems they really sprung this big project on you at the last minute," I said. "Do you think they'd consider giving you an extension on the deadline?" I asked.

"I don't want to ask for one," she admitted. "I've known for several weeks they'd probably want me to do this. I just kept putting it off. It never seemed the right time to get started," she explained. "Actually, all of these things that are coming together at one time to create this stress are things I could have addressed sooner."

As it turns out, she'd known all summer that her daughter would need a physical, but kept forgetting to make the call to schedule an appointment. She wanted to switch to a new doctor, but that would mean choosing the new doctor. She wanted to do research and talk to several people to get opinions before doing that. So rather than making an appointment with the old doctor or making a decision about the new one, she did nothing.

And the car? The "check engine" light in the car had been warning her for over a month that it needed a checkup. But she was waiting on her husband to take it in. Things had been too busy for him lately, so she'd opted to keep driving it until he found the time. The current busyness crisis could have been completely avoided if she'd not kept putting things off for another day. At the core of putting things off was her insistence that certain circumstances come together before she move forward. Perfection was at the core of her procrastination. Not doing it a certain way became an excuse for not doing it at all.

If there is one habit that creates the illusion of busyness, it is procrastination. Many people would not feel so busy if they simply started doing what they know they need to be doing at the moment. Instead, they find other things to do to fill up the time until finally their inner alarm alerts them that they can no longer drag their feet. At that moment a sense of urgency kicks in. "I'm so busy! I don't know how I am going to get all of this done by Friday!" they exclaim.

When I was a teenager, I'd procrastinate whenever it was time to study or write a paper. So I shouldn't have been surprised when the issue reared its head in adulthood—especially once I started writing books. I don't know about you, but the irony is that I actually get a lot done when I procrastinate—files get re-organized, the house gets an extra cleaning, and all sorts of "important" projects suddenly become urgent and finally get tackled. I happily do anything else to avoid tackling the big project on the horizon.

Ultimately, I've learned that there is only one way to overcome procrastination:

Dig your heels in and just do what needs to be done.

Perhaps you procrastinate sometimes and were hoping I had a magic remedy to help you kick your procrastination habit. I don't. The key is to pause in the moment when you are about to avoid the task at hand and redirect your attention to what really matters. Below are five approaches you may find helpful, but at the core of all of them is a simple message: Just do it!

1. Commit five minutes to the task.
This is my favorite technique. Rather than telling yourself that you have to do it all at once, commit to just a small amount of time. Whether it is a major project at work or cleaning the closets, getting started is half the battle. Once you get started, you gain momentum and are more likely to keep going until you reach the finish line.

2. Stop making it a big deal.

One of the biggest reasons we procrastinate is that in our minds, the thing we need to do is such a big deal that it overwhelms us and we get stuck. Paralysis sets in and you instead focus on something you know you can get done (like the laundry or a game of solitaire). Of course, the thing you really need to be doing is nagging you ever so persistently even as you focus elsewhere. Instead of allowing the task before you to be a big deal, make a decision to divide it into manageable pieces. Even if you are procrastinating about a conversation, start by writing down what you want to say (step 1), then establish a time to have the conversation (step 2), then say the words that need to be said (step 3). Small steps are key.

3. Give yourself permission to do it imperfectly.

Another reason many people procrastinate is that they fear they will do it wrong or poorly, so they just don't do it at all. For example, one of the best ways to write a book is to write it as quickly as you can, getting onto paper the thoughts that come to you without regard to style and editing. Then you can go back to revise and polish. If I only wrote when I knew it would be perfect, I'd still be working on my first book! Do you insist that everything be done a certain way? Do you have a hard time relaxing if your house is a mess or if things are out of order? Do you beat yourself up for making mistakes? I've got a simple message for you today: It's time to let go of your perfectionism. It becomes a stumbling block that keeps you stuck. Be willing to do your best, but be willing to do it imperfectly. It frees you to be human and it frees you to make progress.

4. Make it fun.

Ask yourself, "How could I make this fun?" Invite someone to help you with the task you're procrastinating about or find some way to make it enjoyable. When you fully engage in the present moment, you experience the joyful satisfaction of accomplishing the task at hand and procrastination disappears.

5. Drop the goal. Enjoy the day.
No need to pretend that you're going to get it done today if you're not. If you insist on procrastinating, then at the very least, don't tell yourself you're going to get started today. Instead, drop the task from your to-do list for now. This frees your mind to enjoy the present moment without the dreadful feeling that you should be doing something else.

Overcoming procrastination is a process, so don't beat yourself up when you do great one day and then the next day you find yourself engaging in your old habits. Expect that change won't happen overnight. You will transform your bad habits when you persist with your new ones. Expecting to drop your procrastination habit in one fell swoop would be like taking one ice skating lesson and then expecting that you will never fall. Once you have the steps in your mind to overcome procrastination, you must be disciplined enough to keep trying the steps until you get it right.

Procrastination and Your Late Habit

There are a host of "goals" and important activities that many people insist they are too busy to get to. In many of these cases the real issue is not being too busy—it's procrastination. When you procrastinate, the most important tasks pile up and you suddenly feel more busy because you've got less time left to accomplish things you knew needed to be accomplished. It is tempting to insist that if only you had more time, you would be able to get everything done. However, I have discovered that it isn't about how much time you have, but how you use the time you have.

One of the reasons I used to think I was so "busy" was because I was always running late. I hated being late (but not enough to do something about it). It made me feel anxious and, depending on the situation, embarrassed. I regularly found myself apologizing for being late, citing problems with traffic or some other excuse for my delay. Being late was simply a part of my lifestyle. Interestingly, even when I had more time, I was still late—usually about ten to fifteen minutes. If you are regularly late, you are probably late approximately the same amount of time everywhere you go. It may be five minutes, fifteen minutes, or thirty minutes based on your procrastination comfort zone. There is a point at which you feel the pressure and get moving—and it is different for everyone.

One afternoon at a luncheon where an etiquette expert was the featured speaker, I heard a concept that I had honestly never attempted. She said, "Set up your schedule so that you are ten minutes early for every appointment." My lifestyle and approach were so hurried that it had never seriously occurred to me that I could be early for anything. She went on, "When you are late and someone is waiting on you, you are essentially communicating to them that your time is more important than theirs."

"Really?" I thought. I'd never considered it that way, but it's true. My heart sank as I thought about the number of times someone had waited on me because I was late. I never consciously thought, "My time is more important," but that was the underlying message. When someone sits at a restaurant for fifteen minutes waiting on you to arrive because you were too busy to leave on time, you are sending them a message.

Create New Rules for Yourself

Transforming your lifestyle means changing your perspective and shifting your approach to everyday living. For example, when I was in busyness mode, my natural tendency was to do everything as quickly as possible. Even when I planned my travel schedule, it didn't occur to me to give myself as much extra time as possible. When I transitioned out of busyness mode, I created a new rule for traveling to speaking engagements: If the speaking engagement is before 3:00 P.M., arrive the day before. It is a simple rule that does not infringe upon other work responsibilities.

In fact, I am very productive when I arrive in a city the day before an engagement because I am free from the normal distractions of being in the office. With my laptop and cell phone, I can do almost everything I would be able to do if I was in the office. But most important, I have time to relax before the engagement and have no worries about delayed flights or last-minute debacles that could throw me off schedule. This leaves me better rested to inspire the people whom I've traveled to see. It feels good not to wait until the last possible moment to do the things that you have to do.

What new rules do you need to create for yourself that would empower you to stop putting things on hold or risking being late or missing a deadline?

My Challenge to You Today

Get started! Whatever you've been procrastinating about, stop making it a big deal. Break it into manageable pieces and just do it.

Five-Minute Journal

What are you procrastinating about? What is the first step you need to take to get it done? When will you take that step this week?

One-Minute Meditation

I accept that the "right" circumstances are not a necessity for me to get started.

DAY 22

Learn to Manage Your Household— Automate and Delegate!

When asked, "What is the most stressful aspect of your schedule?"—the number one answer was a tie between "work demands" and "keeping up with household chores." Each received 38 percent of the responses. While challenges such as parenting and not having time to exercise were also cited, it is particularly noteworthy that many people find it just as stressful to keep the house in order as it is to deal with the challenges brought on by the demands of working every day.

Because so much of the day for many people is spent away from home, the idea of working some more after arriving home is bleak. As many housewives and stay-at-home parents will attest, you can make a full-time job out of managing a household well. Most have had to opt for an abbreviated version of tasks, but nonetheless, managing your home is essentially your part-time job. While some have a one-person home and shoulder all of the responsibility, others have a spouse or children who can share it. But too often, the responsibility is not shared equitably.

Today, I invite you to think about how your home operates. Is it efficient? Clean? Welcoming? Is the laundry done consistently and regularly? Are your bills paid consistently and in a timely manner? Do you lose bills, keys, invitations, and other items often? Is it normal to run out of household items or groceries? Does everything in your house have a place to be stored? Is it easy to get dinner on the table? Is there a system for communicating schedules, appointments, and messages? In other words:

Does your household have a rhythm that enhances your life?

Or

Does your household serve as a source of

stress and challenges?

Your home is your haven—and it is also your command center. If things are not in order at home, it impacts your productivity in every other area. It affects how well you sleep, your happiness, and your relationships. Of the 55 percent of Busyness Survey respondents who indicated that they have not had a friend visit their home in over two months, some are not only too busy to have friends over, they simply don't want anyone to see how they are living. Things are a mess, and they'd prefer to keep that to themselves.

One of the biggest reasons people experience stress when it comes to household chores is that procrastination leads to many routine activities becoming emergencies. As a result, when something is finally handled, it is because it has to be handled *right now* or something stressful will happen. Here are just a few of the everyday chores that can become emergencies if not handled routinely. How many of these have become emergencies for you?

- ☐ Run out of clean socks, shirts, underwear, or some item of clothing you want to wear on that day
- ☐ Miss an invitation because you didn't open the mail
- ☐ Pay a bill late because you lost it or didn't get to it in time
- ☐ Had an appliance break because it was not maintained well
- ☐ Had a messy kitchen or living room when someone dropped by unexpectedly
- ☐ Ran out of a food item you needed in order to cook a meal and had to run to the grocery store at the last minute

How much easier would your day-to-day life be if your chores took less time and effort? With the increasingly hectic pace of many lives, we hear the phrase "simplify your life" more often. Simplifying can be good, and I'd like to suggest something just as important—making your life easier. You know, those simple but time-consuming household tasks you have to do week after week or month after month, such as grocery shopping, cooking, cleaning, running errands, and paying bills? Wouldn't it make your life easier to make those things less of a burden on your time? Well, here are seven strategies for managing your household more effectively and cutting down on the amount of time and effort you must expend on a day-to-day basis:

1. Have a central communication center.

A household "communication center" is a central location for basic household management. Your communication center is a place for your household calendar—with dates and appointments for everyone in the house as well as any household maintenance appointments such as reminders for cutting the grass, spring cleaning, and so forth. Here is where you should expect to find phone messages, keys, or "Went to the store, will be back at 2" notes. The communication center is where you might shred junk mail and open and file important mail, pay bills, or sign permission slips if you have children in school. Having a household communication center is a strategy that keeps you and everyone else organized by giving you a structure and a place to conduct business pertaining to everyday living.

Whether it's a desk in the den, a spot in the kitchen, or a corner of the entry, set up your communication center in a place that is easily accessible to everyone. Having it located somewhere that you and everyone in the house have a reason to pass by on a daily basis makes it effortless and functional for all.

2. Don't let chores pile up.

Of those interviewed who do not feel positively about the state of their household, many echoed a similar theme: You can't let chores pile up. "You've got to stay on top of it," said one single mom. "Don't let mail sit unopened, leave the kitchen untidy at night, or try to wash clothes just once a week because once it piles up, it's just too much and it stresses you out because it weighs heavily on your mind." Tackle chores after work on Fridays and keep Saturday to yourself, she advised. The bottom line is, there are many things you may not feel like doing, but if you don't do them, life can become unnecessarily busy.

Remember the concept, "Stop so you can catch up"? It is an important step for you to embrace as you take greater control of managing your home. Set aside some time to handle the tasks you've been putting off. Take out your calendar and schedule some time to do it this week. If the main issue is cleaning the house and you don't have time, consider hiring a maid service to get things in order. Then you will have a fresh start to begin handling chores as they come. And remember that an important element of your 28-day plan is creating enough space in your life to handle all that comes at you. That, of course, means that you must make sure to build in time in your everyday activities to be able to do that. When you are always in a hurry to get things done, it is more likely that you will not clean as you go, respond to messages as they come, answer mail when it arrives, fix a leaky faucet when it first starts having problems, and so forth. All of the lessons your mother probably tried to teach you when you were a kid apply here: Clean as you go, put things back where you got them, and don't ignore problems because they only get worse.

3. Create a printed shopping list.

One reason many people go to the grocery store repeatedly is because they didn't remember to put an item on their list when they shopped a day or two earlier. If you buy fresh produce (and since you are focused on eating well as part of your self-care plan, let's assume that you do), you will need to go to the store more often than someone who doesn't. But you should still be able to limit your trips to once a week at a day and time that is convenient for you. Type a list of all of the items that you shop for on a regular basis and print out multiple copies. Keep copies in the kitchen or your household communication center, and take out a blank one each week. As you (or your family members) notice items you need, circle them. When it's time to go shopping, you'll be organized and less likely to miss items that end up making for quick trips later.

Of course, if you order your groceries online and have them delivered, you could save even more time. Use technology to your advantage. Today, find out if you have the option of online grocery shopping in your area. If you do, you can eliminate a major chore from your list altogether. Online grocers typically save your previous shopping lists and also allow you to use coupons if you have them, making it easier for you to reorder items that you regularly buy, and making your shopping experience quick and efficient.

4. Automate your bill paying.

This is one area in which you should take full advantage of technology. In most cases there is no need to write a check to pay a bill anymore. If you dread sitting down to pay bills, make a decision to stop doing it! Set your accounts up to be automatically paid out of your checking account once a month. Most companies are glad to set up this service for you, or you can set it up automatically through your bank. Even if you do not have the option of setting up an automatic withdrawal, or if a bill is just a one-time occurrence, many banks and credit unions offer you the option of having them print and send checks on your behalf from your online account. It's like having your own personal bookkeeper. This is an easy delegation. Once you have your accounts set up, it can take you literally a matter of seconds to pay bills. If you haven't already automated your bill paying, plan to set up that option for yourself immediately.

5. Prepare your meals once per week, or hire a personal chef to do it for you.

If you spend a couple of hours once each week preparing enough meals for the whole week, you'll not only save time but find yourself under a lot less pressure as the week goes on. In some cities you'll find meal preparation studios where you go for one to two hours and prepare up to two weeks' worth of meals. You bring them home, put them in the freezer, and take them out when you are ready to cook them. Start with these Web sites: www.dreamdinners.com and www.supersuppers.com. If you don't have the time to do it yourself and you can afford it, consider hiring someone else to do it. Having your own personal cook may be much less expensive than you think. Imagine, someone to shop, cook, package, and store your meals in the refrigerator or freezer—and even clean up the mess! Visit www.personalchef.com to find one in your area.

6. Have a reserve.

A reserve is an important element of self-care because it allows you to relax knowing that you have a margin of error when things don't go quite as planned. Having a reserve means having more than you need so that you have a cushion for emergencies—whether minor or major. Money typically comes to mind when one thinks of a reserve, but for purposes of managing your household, also consider keeping a reserve of everyday items such as water, paper towels, toiletries, or lightbulbs. When you have a reserve, running out of things—a major household stressor—becomes far less likely.

7. Don't do it all yourself. Delegate!

If you live with other people, including children, you should not be responsible for every chore in the household. Even if you have children who are just six or seven years old, teach and expect them to clean up after themselves. If you can manage it in your budget, hire people to help you with the things you dislike doing—whether it is yard work, cleaning, or repairs. If there are other adults in the household, have a conversation about how to share the responsibilities realistically. Keep in mind what is most convenient for each person based on their schedule and other duties. If you lean toward being a perfectionist, keep in mind that others may not do it perfectly—and that is okay. The goal here is not perfection, but self-care and having time for the people and things that matter most to you.

My Challenge to You Today

Take control of your household routine! Choose one action from the seven listed above to implement today. Schedule the others that apply on future dates on your calendar.

Five-Minute Journal

What aspect of my household management is causing me stress? What could I do to alleviate that stress long term?

One-Minute Meditation

My household has a rhythm that enhances the flow of my life.

DAY 23

Respect the Pace of Others

It seems like so many people don't even have time to be courteous anymore. In traffic, at stores, in public—it's all about getting what you want when you want it. That makes me sad.

—JANET, 27

While I was walking in front of my mother and then twelve-year-old brother through the maze at the security screening area at Washington Dulles Airport a couple of years ago, my mother called to me, "Val, let's stop so that we can let this man by." I turned to see a hurried, forty-something man squeeze by in a huff. "Thank you," he said, looking annoyed. We had been walking at a reasonable pace, and I was careful not to walk too fast because my mother needs to carefully concentrate to remain balanced while she is walking. A brain aneurysm in 2001 and resulting brain surgery initially stole nearly all of her physical abilities—walking, talking, standing, swallowing, and seeing clearly. Today, by grace, she has recovered all of those abilities, but walking and talking still take more effort for her than for the average person.

"He was nearly breathing down my neck," my mom said after

the man passed, "and he kept murmuring loud enough for me to hear him, 'This woman is holding up everybody. I wish she would hurry up!'" A few seconds later I found myself right behind him, waiting patiently as he "held everybody up" to get his laptop unpacked for the security screening machine. I looked him in the eye and calmly said, "My mother had a brain aneurysm. She is disabled and simply cannot walk as fast as the rest of us. We're all in a hurry, but we don't have to be rude to one another." He looked at me, speechless, but made no response.

I was fuming, but I didn't show it. Ironically, as I reflected on those few brief moments, I recognized that I, too, have had moments when I was easily annoyed with the slower pace of others without considering what they might be going through. While I was tempted to judge him, I had to take a closer look at myself. It can be so tempting for us to get impatient with others, especially when we are stressed or feel rushed. Today, I want to remind you to have mercy on those who seem to make your life "inconvenient" in some way. Perhaps it is someone in your office who rubs you the wrong way, or the person driving in front of you who does not move as quickly as you'd like. Take a deep breath. Be patient. In fact, go a step beyond patience and choose kindness. You never know what others are dealing with. Don't be too busy to care.

In a world where most of us feel the pressure of life's hectic pace on a daily basis, it can be easy to operate as though your goals, challenges, and concerns are all that matter. That neighbor who always seems to be in a bad mood may be dealing with an abusive spouse. The clerk who seems rude may be mourning the loss of a loved one. The coworker who doesn't get work done as fast as you do just might not be as talented and quick as you. You never know what others are going through. And even if they are not dealing with anything at all, give others a break.

Have mercy. Be patient. Practice kindness. Give people the benefit of the doubt. Be civil to those who cross your path. Following these rules of kindness will lead you to consistently interact with people in a way that alleviates the stress that can be tempting to take out on others when your plate is full.

MY CHALLENGE TO YOU TODAY

When you find yourself easily annoyed or impatient today, take a deep breath and make a decision to be patient and kind.

FIVE-MINUTE JOURNAL

When do I find myself easily annoyed or impatient? What could I do to replace annoyance and impatience with kindness and patience?

ONE-MINUTE MEDITATION

My goal today is to practice patience and respect the pace of others.

DAY : **24**

Being Busy ≠
Being Significant

Honestly, I'm not that busy anymore. I've designed
my life that way and I like it. I am making more of
an impact than ever because I have time to invest in
my family and myself.

—SARAH, 53

After I began my journey to transform my busy lifestyle into a
healthy one that embraces self-care, I noticed that the struggle
to stay on track was intense. My intentions were good, but there
was a strong pull toward filling up my days that I could not explain. I had identified and addressed my fears at the start of my
journey, yet it seemed that a weightier fear persisted. I knew that
if I did not peel back the layers to explore the root cause, I would
not be able to effect a permanent and lasting shift. It would be
a constant tug-of-war, a spiritual battle between my ego, whose
appetite demanded more, more, more, and my spirit, which
screamed less *is* more!

The journey of change is often a multiphased one. We cannot see all of our needs, issues, and potential obstacles when we
begin the journey. The farther along we travel, the more we discover. We make small changes and those lead to bigger ones. We

make a shift in one area and find out that as a result, we must adjust in another area. I think this happens for a purpose. If you knew up front all that you would have to address in order to change, it would probably be too overwhelming. So our changes unfold just a little at a time. As you succeed in your changes, it reveals more, but only as much as you can handle.

As you face new challenges on your journey, listen for new clues that will lead to an opportunity for growth. That's what I did when I sensed an unexplained fear holding me back. I started asking questions. I didn't know the answers intellectually, but I trusted that they would come. When I got quiet and listened, they did come. This was a breakthrough to lasting change!

Why am I so afraid to not be busy? I pondered one evening while taking a break outdoors. What do I think it says about me to not be busy? I quieted down to hear my answer. Part of me wanted to believe that I really didn't know. But as a coach and personally, I have found "I don't know" to usually be a cop-out. It's the easy thing to say—and it's quick. I do know the answer, I told myself. But did I want to hear it? Not really, because I was unsure of what I would do with the information once I learned it.

But before I could continue my reasoning, the answer came to me: You are afraid that if you are not busy, you are not important. More specifically, you are not significant. You think being busy equals being significant, and therefore, if you slow down and stop taking on so much, you won't be special and important. I was stunned to hear this thought. Is this true? Is this really what I think? I took a deep breath and sat for a moment, and realized that the lightbulb had come on. It was absolutely what I thought. And it motivated me subconsciously to stay busy, even as I was trying to change my life.

So what would I do with that information? I knew logically that it wasn't true, but that didn't change how I *felt*. Until that point I had not realized it, but my emotions were driving my life. I was fulfilling a need to be significant—or rather a need to *feel* significant. But I already was significant, and so are you. You are significant because you are here. Your significance is not something you earn through good works and busyness. It is something you are born with. Your life has a purpose. You are uniquely gifted, passionate, and equipped to touch people in a way that only you can. But if you don't feel it, you will behave in ways that sabotage what is already true.

Perhaps this is not your exact scenario, but there may be something else. It may stem from deeply buried feelings and false beliefs about yourself, stemming as far back as your childhood. Did you have to work to earn love and accolades? Did you get attention when you were busy, but were scolded for having too much fun? Were you always waiting for someone to say, "I'm proud of you," but rarely heard it? Was it all work and no play in your house? Are you busy trying to make up for something you did or didn't do? Are you placing unattainable expectations on yourself in your job, your relationships, as a parent? Are you aiming to feel needed, or to help others see how much they need you or how irreplaceable you are—in other words, how significant you are? Whatever the issue, at its core you may be seeking to feel something that you don't otherwise feel—significance, importance, or recognition. The problem is that being busy does not deliver that. Instead, it becomes a substitute. When we attach a meaning to being busy, it becomes our justification for our actions. "I *have* to do this," we say. But we should finish the sentence, ". . . in order to satisfy my need to feel significant."

Justifying Busyness with Judgment

Equating busyness with significance has been a human instinct since time began. Even the Bible contains an age-old story about this issue—the story of two sisters, Mary and Martha. Martha opened her home to Jesus and was busy the entire time, preparing for his visit. Meanwhile, Mary sat at Jesus' feet from the moment he walked in the door, listening to all he had to say. Martha was irritated and spoke up. Read what happens:

> As Jesus and his disciples were on their way, he came to a village where a woman named Martha opened her home to him. She had a sister called Mary, who sat at the Lord's feet listening to what he said. But Martha was distracted by all the preparations that had to be made. She came to him and asked, "Lord, don't you care that my sister has left me to do the work myself? Tell her to help me!"
>
> "Martha, Martha," the Lord answered, "you are worried and upset about many things, but few things are needed— or indeed only one. Mary has chosen what is better, and it will not be taken away from her."
>
> (LUKE 10:39–42)

"What is better" refers to the text that is referenced prior to the story, the parable of the Good Samaritan, which says: "Love the Lord your God with all your heart and with all your soul and with all your strength and with all your mind, and love your neighbor as yourself."

This exchange between Martha, Mary, and Jesus illustrates an attitude that is prevalent today. Martha's attitude was to focus on what she felt needed to be done to prepare for the visit, thereby missing the opportunity to connect with the one she loved right there in the present moment. But if we delve deeper, we can see that Martha really wanted recognition for her busyness. She essentially said, "Look at me! I'm doing all this work! See, I know what's important here! Lazy Mary is over there doing nothing. Tell her she's wrong!" But Jesus did not. Martha wanted to justify her choices by judging Mary's.

The underlying message is, I'm the one who is sacrificing and I should be acknowledged for it. Have you ever felt that way? Mary, unlike Martha, used the time to listen and learn. She soaked up all that Jesus had to say. It appears she understood the gravity of the opportunity before her that day—and cooking, cleaning, and preparing were not going to distract her from that opportunity. She wasn't focused on doing anything, but being fully present in the moment.

Use the following questions to get honest with yourself about your busyness habit. I have divided the questions into the five key areas of your life. There are questions for each area. Feel free to add other questions that come to you and are relevant to your circumstances. Use these as a self-curiosity tool to discover ways in which you may be equating busyness with significance or importance, and to better understand what makes you feel authentically significant so that you can create more of that feeling in your life without creating more activity. You may think you aren't, but answer these questions with an open mind to determine if there is an opportunity for you to further grow and solidify your shift to a healthy, self-care lifestyle that doesn't compel you to keep doing more and more.

RELATIONSHIPS

- Do you spend time doing things for loved ones or friends so that they will approve of you, think better of you, or treat you better? How does this make you feel? What would make you feel more empowered in these situations?

- For parents: Do you do things for your children out of fear that not doing them will mean that you are a bad parent, or to make them like you more? What feelings are you trying to manufacture when this occurs?

- What makes you feel significant, important, or recognized (choose the verb that resonates most with you) in your relationship with the loved ones who are closest to you?

WORK

- Do you take on work that is not your responsibility? Why? What rule could you create for yourself to stop taking on the work of others?

- What are you striving for at work? What need will it fill for you?

- What makes you feel authentically significant in your work?

MONEY

- In what ways are money and significance connected in your mind? How does that impact how you feel about your personal financial circumstances?

- Do you waste time digging yourself into debt or overspending on items that make you feel important or cause others to "recognize" you?

- How could you use your money to create a legacy of true significance?

- *What message do you think your busyness habit is offering you right now?*
- *In what ways, if any, are you busy trying to prove yourself worthy or deserving of blessings and good fortune?*

HEALTH & PHYSICAL ENVIRONMENTS

- *What clutters your environment that is not an authentic representation of you, but gives you a feeling of significance, importance, or recognition?*
- *What will it take for you to find wholeness and healing from any issues related to subconsciously equating busyness with significance?*

Don't be afraid to delve deep to find your answers. Once you have an understanding of what is driving you toward busyness, you can step forward in courage and address the issue. After I peeled back the layers to discover a lingering issue that was so deeply embedded I didn't even know it was there, I began to face it. One step at a time, I began noticing the ways in which I used busyness to feel significant. And when those moments occurred, I made choices that sometimes caused me to feel very uncomfortable. My natural inclination was to feed the insecurity, but I learned to stand firm.

When asked to serve on a worthwhile committee that would be visible and interesting, yet time-consuming and out of alignment with my vision, I declined. When regular opportunities to fill too many weekends with speaking engagements became a regular occurrence, I learned to set limits to my schedule in order to enjoy plenty of quality time with my family and friends—because weekends are when *they* are available. Over time, you will build your strength by taking actions based on what you know to be true about your own significance rather than succumbing to temptations based on how you feel.

MY CHALLENGE TO YOU TODAY

Be honest with yourself. With just a few more chapters to go, is there still an internal struggle that compels you to choose busyness over self-care? Make a decision to get to the bottom of it. Answer the questions in this chapter, and even talk it out with friends, a coach, or a counselor if that helps.

FIVE-MINUTE JOURNAL

What is the last issue you need to conquer in order to permanently change your approach? What is at the core of this issue? What truth do you need to embrace? What change will you make as a result?

ONE-MINUTE MEDITATION

My significance stems from who I am and not from what I do.

DAY 25

Allow Space for What You Want

I have such a hard time saying no that even when my intentions are good, I seem to eventually fill up my free time with things to do that keep me from having time for myself.

—LESLIE, 33

Often, busy people insist that there is nothing they can drop from their schedule. It's all important, and they are the only ones who can do most of it, so there is just no way to solve the problem. Perhaps you cannot see how to clear your plate right now, but that doesn't mean it can't be done. If you are open and willing to make adjustments, and possibly major changes in a few key areas, you will see a powerful transformation in how you live. Imagine yourself for a moment, having time for the aspects of life that matter most while also meeting your financial and emotional needs. Imagine your days filled with meaningful work, joyful activities, rest, fun, and enough time margin that you don't have to race from one commitment to the next.

There are likely some activities and habits in your life that consume your time and energy but do not offer equal benefit to you. During these 28 days, it's time to eliminate those activities. Take a step toward ridding your schedule of activities and routines that no longer serve you. What activity will you let go of or modify?

Here are a few examples of the types of habits and activities I am referring to:

- *Committees or other meetings that take a lot of time*
- *Something you agreed to do begrudgingly*
- *Any activity that requires a lot of effort without yielding equivalent results (unproductive)*
- *Any activity that serves no meaningful purpose in your life*
- *Watching television excessively*
- *Things you are trying to force to happen*
- *Going places you don't want to be (parties, shopping with a difficult or negative friend, gatherings with people you don't want to be around, etc.)*
- *Doing things simply because they've always been done*

I was working with a man who was struggling to make space in his life for his vision, and I began to ask him a series of questions to help him get to the core of why it was difficult for him to say "no" to new activities and readjust his approach to ongoing ones. The conversation went something like this.

"Why are you afraid to make big changes in how you approach your life?" I asked. "Specifically, why is it so difficult for you to stop scheduling new activities on your already busy schedule?"

"It took a long time for me to build this business," he explained. "For the first few years I was just barely hanging on. Any opportunities that crossed my path, I took advantage of.

My schedule was wide open. It wasn't a problem of having too much to do, but having too little. So I spent much of my time marketing to get the business going. Then business was no longer a trickle, but a steadier stream although not as lucrative as I'd hoped. I worked more, improving the business and services. Now I've turned a corner: I have started to turn down business! But not nearly enough. I'll block out vacation time, but if a big piece of business comes along or some other opportunity, I budge on the vacation time. Before you know it, the time that was blocked out is filled in. It wouldn't be so bad if it happened just once. But I am coming to recognize that it is a compulsion. First my assistant warned me to stop taking on so much. Now my wife is telling me it's getting out of control. But I don't know how to stop."

"So part of what I am hearing is that you've done a lot of things right and now you are getting the kinds of opportunities you once hoped for? You're a victim of your own success."

"Yes."

"What are you afraid will happen if you stop taking on business and opportunities that interfere with your ability to have the free time you say you want?" I asked.

He was silent for a long time. "I'm almost afraid to answer the question because I like to think of myself as someone who doesn't succumb to fear," he admitted. "And that's making it hard to sort out."

"Okay. I can see how that could happen," I assured him, having felt that way before myself. "But what's the first answer that comes to mind—the one that hits you right in your gut?" Speaking from the gut, his answers began to pour forth.

"I am afraid that if I say 'no' to business, that it will all come to an end," he said. "I am afraid that I don't have the luxury of saying no. There are no guarantees that this time next year, companies will still be calling on me to help them! I feel like I better take advantage of every opportunity while it is here."

"So you are basically afraid that one day business will dry up, and then what would you do?"

"Yeah, what would I do then?" He mirrored the question back to me. Then it occurred to him to answer it. "Hmm. What would I do if it all came to an end?" he pondered aloud. It was a pivotal question for him. "Well, logically this fear really doesn't make any sense." I could hear the lightbulb coming on. "Ever since I started the business, it has grown each year. Why would people suddenly stop buying from me if they are happy with my services? *And they are.* I make sure of it. It's not a particularly rational thought," he admitted. "But I've held to it for a long time. If for any reason the business suddenly failed, it would make me sad. I love what I do. But I would find a way to bounce back. Permanent failure is not an option."

While talking it through, he realized that the fear (his business suddenly failing) that was driving him to do more and more wasn't a rational one. Out of this realization, he began looking at the specifics of his vision. He clarified how much business he would need in order to be truly happy and provide for his family—and how much work it would require to handle that amount of business. Anything more than that was optional only if certain criteria were present:

- *The project would not interfere with his vacation time, weekends off, or evenings at home.*
- *It was a project of particular interest to him and would advance his business in some specific way.*
- *It could be accomplished without struggle.*
- *The profit from the project was compelling.*

With these criteria in place, he was now equipped with a plan that allowed room in his life for personal time that was balanced and fulfilling. But first he had to deal with the issues that were keeping him from creating the space for his vision. His struggle reflects the issue we discussed on Day 4, Face Your Fear. Throughout your process of adapting a self-care lifestyle, fear-based choices will present themselves.

Let's consider your model again. That's your vision from the exercise on Day 2 in which you acknowledged where you were, took an inventory, and created a model of what you want your life to look like. So how do you allow space for what you really want?

1. Identify the fear that compels you to say "yes" when you need to say "no."

Getting to the core of your fear will empower you to face it. Imagine yourself in the moment when the opportunity comes along to fill up some free time. You know you should say "no" because you've decided that you need this time for you. But you are so used to saying "yes" and the time is open, and it couldn't hurt just this once, could it? In that moment, what are you afraid will happen if you say "no"?

2. Ask yourself, "What if my fear came true? Then what?"

One of the most empowering actions you can take to overcome your fear is to answer the "what if" questions that race through your mind. You know those questions: What if I fail? What if I'm wrong? What if I make a mistake? What if I miss out on something? Answer the questions for yourself. Then determine what you would do if your "what if" questions came true.

3. Create margin in your life.

Part of creating space is having a buffer that protects you from emergencies and mistakes in your schedule. I call this buffer "margin." It is the space between appointments, the extra time you give yourself to finish a project, or even the rule you create that keeps you from letting your fuel gauge ever end up on empty. The tendency for overloaded, overdriven people is to schedule their lives back-to-back. If you are suddenly stuck in traffic and late for an appointment, you are running so close that it throws off the entire day. Give yourself more time than you need for everything you have to do.

4. Keep your vision in front of you.

One of the main reasons many people fill up their lives with ac-tivities and responsibilities that keep them from the vision is be-cause they simply forget about it. They read a book such as this one, write a vision, get excited about it, then go back to business as usual. I keep a copy of my vision inside a drawer that I open several times a day. I don't have to remember to look at it—I see it every time I open that drawer! It prompts the question, "Are you on track?" The vision is always in the back of my mind. And when opportunities come along to add more to my plate, I am reminded of my vision and automatically filter these opportuni-ties through the criteria I set in my vision. What would be an ef-fective way for you to keep your vision in front of you? Take a moment now to implement your simple reminder.

5. Let go of the thing you are holding tightly.

If you are holding on to something too tightly, it's time to ad-dress the issues behind it. When you are afraid to let go of some-thing that takes up too much space to allow room for your vision, your job is to get to the root of the problem. What are you afraid will happen if you let go? What if you let go anyway? What circumstances could you create that would prove better for you? What would be the first step toward making that happen?

6. Get comfortable with having nothing to do.

One of the reasons that a person's available time gets filled up is that they are uncomfortable with open space. When you have been used to being busy, having time on your hands can make you anxious. It will feel unnatural to you and the automatic response is to create what you are used to—busyness. As you create space in your life, expect it to feel uncomfortable at first.

7. Build your boundary-setting muscles.

This is essential, yet not always easy. You can be strong at setting boundaries in one area of your life, yet pathetic in another. This was my predicament. I set strong boundaries in relationships—able to speak up for myself, give and receive respect, and draw the line on a multitude of issues. Start building your boundary-setting muscles by giving yourself guidelines for when it is appropriate to say "yes." Make a list of criteria. And don't be shy about telling people you'll get back to them. You don't have to make quick decisions. But you do need to make wise ones that give you space for what you truly want in your life.

MY CHALLENGE TO YOU TODAY

Create space for what you want. Identify the thing you've been hesitating to let go of. Refuse to allow it to crowd your schedule and your vision any longer. Take the step you know you need to take to let go.

Five-Minute Journal

In what ways are you crowding the space you need in order to realize your vision? What are you willing to do about it? And when?

What would be an effective way for you to keep your vision in front of you? Take a moment now to implement your simple reminder.

One-Minute Meditation

I am joyfully making space in my life for what I really want.

DAY : **26**

Stop Striving,
Start Trusting

> I've noticed that I'm most productive when I
> go with the flow without trying to force things to
> happen out of timing.
>
> —Iris, 47

We're often busy because we create work for ourselves and impose unnecessary expectations. Too many people are busy laboring in vain—working on projects and engaging in activities that hold no true purpose for their lives. In all that you do, it is essential to have clarity of purpose—a deeper meaning for why you are here and what you are here to do—not only in your everyday life, but for your broader life as well. It is important to recognize that everything in life has a season, and when a season is up, it is important to move on. When it is time to wait, it is essential that you wait. And when it is time for a change, you must trust that your path will unfold in the right way.

Often those who are busy trying to force things to happen do not maximize the opportunities right before them. They are always looking to pursue opportunities rather than attract them. It's called striving—and it can be exhausting. Striving is about making things happen, reaching externally for "the next big thing" to happen rather than walking your unique path and trusting the right opportunities to cross your path.

It is exciting that we don't have to know all of the right answers in our lives in order to do the thing that's best for us. You have an inner guide that wants to lead you onto the right path. I'm sure you've heard that inner voice speak to you or felt at peace about something and moved forward on it. Or maybe it wasn't peace you felt, but turmoil, telling you it was time to make a change. I know that voice to be the Holy Spirit. On many occasions when I have been unsure, I have been led in the right direction where my path unfolded in just the right way.

It was a morning like any other one in November 2000. I dragged myself out of bed, but it felt like I'd just gotten there. I'd attended a reception the night before, and like many nights, there was very little time between walking through the door and getting ready for bed. I was exhausted, but that was irrelevant. I needed to get to the office early to finish preparing for a 9:00 A.M. client meeting. I didn't used to dread work, but it had gotten to that point. I'd lost my excitement for it. Work was starting to feel like *work*. For another day I would bury my feelings, put on my game face, and be grateful for having not just a job, but a business of my own.

I walked into the bathroom to brush my teeth. That was always my transition time from half consciousness to being wide awake. When I finished, I turned on the shower, waited until the water was warm, and stepped in. "Ahhhh," I sighed as the water ran over my back. A moment of relaxation. I took a deep breath—and exhaled. That's when emotion overwhelmed me very suddenly. I tried to control it, but the emotion was too strong. My chest ached in frustration at the day ahead. Tears poured forth. I simply couldn't hold it in any longer. I couldn't pretend any longer.

"I don't want to go to work," I thought. "I don't want to do this anymore." It was my moment of truth. I had ignored my feelings for several months in hopes that I would grow out of it. I stood there crying in the shower, unsure of what the next move was, but positive that it was time for a change. I sensed in my spirit a release—and assurance that if I followed the desires of my heart, everything would work out somehow.

"It would certainly be easier to stay where I am," I thought, afraid of making a change and uncertain of how to do it. In some ways I also felt that I didn't have a right to make a change. I had made a choice to start a business, so I should stick with it. It's flaky to change careers, a voice of reason echoed in my head, especially when you're going to take a drop in income to do it. On this particular morning my spirit spoke loudly through my emotions: "It's time to move on." It wasn't the first time in recent months I'd sensed that bit of wisdom. This time I listened.

My public relations firm required too much personal energy not to be my passion. My passion is what I do now—inspiring people to live more fulfilling, less stressful lives. Now that I was clear on that purpose, any work outside of it felt burdensome. It kept me busy—very busy—but not happy. That morning I decided that whatever it took, I would make a change. Prior to that, fear had controlled my choice. It paralyzed me as a host of fearful questions flooded my mind:

"What if I'm wrong and this is the wrong choice?"

"What if I fail on my new path? Wouldn't it just be better to do well with what I've already started?"

"What if I can't make a good living at it? I mean, I like my condo and I like to eat, but those things cost money, you know?"

"What will people think? How will I explain my bold choice?" In the end I figured out that it was a bold choice in *my* mind, but the world wouldn't stop spinning because Valorie Burton was changing careers. Everyone else has their own stuff to think about. We often think "they" are so concerned with what we do. But they aren't, so it's important to note that the inner critics are often heard more clearly than the external ones.

After that morning I recognized that a life busy with work or activities that do not fulfill you may look full, but it is empty. I made a drastic change in my life. I transitioned out of my old career and into a new one. The first step was the most important—I made a decision to do it. With a few unpleasant exceptions, nothing changes in your schedule until you make a decision to change it.

The bigger lesson is that when it is time to make a change, it's time to make a change. There is no getting around it. You may be at a stage where your spirit is nudging you. Or like me, you may be at a stage where your spirit is screaming for a change. When you stay in a situation—whether personal or professional—longer than you are meant to, you become busy but no longer fruitful because you are engaging in work, relationships, and activities that no longer hold your destiny. When your time is finished in a situation, gracefully and boldly move on to the next horizon. Rather than trying to keep something going or make things happen, trust that whatever is next for you will unfold in the right timing. Your fruitfulness and productivity will follow.

Embrace the Wait

While returning from a speaking engagement in Minneapolis on an evening flight, I heard the pilot announce that he expected we would land a few minutes early. Instead, as we approached the Washington, DC, area, nearby thunderstorms changed the plan. For more than an hour—as daylight turned to evening—we circled northern Virginia. At first I found myself—like many of the passengers—feeling agitated. Then I took a deep breath, closed my eyes, and enjoyed a few moments of rest.

I've noticed that so often in life, when we encounter a holding pattern, the natural reaction is one of frustration for having to wait. But a holding pattern serves a greater purpose—protecting you until the right conditions unfold that allow you to land at your destination safely. In our fast-paced world, we are tempted to believe that faster is always better. Sometimes, though, pushing for something to happen in the wrong timing can unnecessarily force you into a storm. It creates unnecessary chaos and commotion in your life.

In what area of your life do you feel as though you are in a holding pattern? It could be a relationship, your finances, career, or health. Perhaps it's time to relax and practice patience while you wait. Waiting may be your gift in disguise. Take a deep breath, trust divine timing, and calmly embrace the journey.

My Challenge to You Today

Get in sync with the right timing. Rather than causing yourself unnecessary stress and busywork by striving to make things happen, start trusting that your life will unfold just as it should, just when it should.

Five-Minute Journal

In what ways are you striving rather than trusting? How is your approach causing you frustration? Will you relax, and when?

One-Minute Meditation

I trust that my life will unfold in divine timing.

DAY 27

Don't Fight Every Battle

Drama can be the biggest time-waster.
—NICOLE, 27

Some issues simply do not deserve your time. Getting caught up in personal battles, attempts to change people, and other fruitless efforts are a tremendous waste of your time and contribute significantly to a busy lifestyle. When you regularly get sucked into arguments—even petty ones—you have less energy to handle the things that matter and you are less likely to connect with the very people you love.

A woman told me recently, "If I could just get my husband to stop leaving his wet towels on the floor after he takes a shower . . . and if I could just get him to stop letting my three-year-old leave *his* towels on the floor, I would feel like he was contributing more to keeping the house clean."

"How long has your husband been doing this?" I asked.

"Well, since we've been married," she admitted. "That's seven years."

"Hmm. And you've asked him to put his towels away?" I probed.

"Every day!" she exclaimed. "He'll do it for a couple of days, and then it's right back to the same problem. He's a great husband in so many ways, but this issue with the towels drives me crazy. It would be so easy for him to just pick them up and put them in the laundry basket!"

I could sense her frustration. "So you've tried to get him to change and he hasn't. What's the likelihood that he's going to stop this annoying habit?" I asked.

"He probably won't," she said.

I looked at her as she processed what she had said. "He's probably not going to change, and this is not life-or-death, so maybe I need to change how I look at it," she continued.

"So basically, you have three choices," I suggested. "One, accept the towels on the floor as something you choose to live with. Two, consider 'putting towels away' to just be one of your daily chores. Or three, be irritated every day. Which one sounds best to you?" I asked.

It was in that moment that a lightbulb came on for her. "Well, it would only take me a few seconds to just pick up the towels and put them in the laundry basket," she said. "I'll just do it. I don't think it's worth any more fussing and negative energy. I will just think of it as one of the things I do."

Stop Trying to Change People

Our conversation was a simple illustration of how you can allow the things you cannot change to become a source of unnecessary frustration—sometimes for years. As you may have learned in your own life, you cannot change people. If you base your peace and level of happiness on the attitudes and actions of others, you will find yourself being consistently disappointed. I am not suggesting that you stop speaking up for yourself and making reasonable requests of others. I am suggesting, however, that you don't become so attached to your need for them to change that you stress yourself out unnecessarily.

Have the courage to accept the things (no matter how large or small) you cannot change and the courage to change what you can. Here's how:

1. Accept the people in your life as they are.

As difficult as it may be at times, it is absolutely essential in a loving relationship to accept a person for who he or she is. Think back to a time when you did not feel accepted. How did it make you feel? Accepting a person for who they are does not mean condoning bad behavior. It means accepting what is and building from there rather than requiring a person to change in order for them to receive love, kindness, or approval from you.

2. Ask yourself, "In what ways could I respond differently in relationships in which I wish the other person would change?"

Some people know how to push your buttons—and they'll do it as often as they can in order to get the reaction they want from you. Others are not trying to push buttons, but inevitably do, as they do things that displease you. Change the dynamic of a situation by choosing a new response. In the case of the conversation I just outlined, the woman simply determined that something as simple as towels on the floor was not worth the frustration and negativity. So she let it go! "He's probably not going to change. It's just not important to him, so I guess I will have to be the one to change unless I want to keep feeling frustrated." Choose your battles wisely. What do you need to let go of?

3. Are there boundaries I need to set to protect myself?

It is sometimes necessary to set clear boundaries and protect them. For example, I don't permit "drama" in my life. I do not allow people and situations that are negative, messy, or lacking in integrity into my life. I just don't have time for them. When I see such situations or people coming, I make it clear that certain conversations, situations, and approaches are not acceptable to me and I won't take part. What boundaries do you need to set to keep peace, joy, and serenity in your life? What conversations do you need to have to make those boundaries clear to people who have stepped across them?

4. Have I met the other person's request for change?

It can be easy to expect change in others without noticing that others would like to see a change in us as well. Be willing to take others' requests for change seriously. Rather than being offended, be honest with yourself. Perhaps it is time to make a change. When you are willing to change for someone else, they will often let down their wall and meet your requests, too. If you are the one who must take the first step, do it. Sometimes we must let go of the need to be right in order to embrace the opportunity for peace, joy, and love.

Stop Fighting Unnecessary Battles

Do you sometimes feel as though you are constantly fighting battles? Whether at work, at home, or with the rude clerk in the checkout line, make a decision not to fight every time. There are points in our lives when it feels like the world is against us. It can be natural to put up your defenses and head into battle. But if you stay in that mode, you will find yourself fighting so often that you will be worn out and continually frustrated. So how do you know which battles to fight? Ask yourself one simple question: Will the outcome of this battle matter a year from now? If the answer is no, let the battle work itself out and save yourself the energy and stress.

Don't Take Things Personally

Several years ago a friend of mine said, "Valorie, the rude or hurtful things a person may say or do to you have nothing to do with you." I was perplexed by her assertion. How is it possible that someone else's negative behavior toward me isn't about me? She went on to explain, "It's about the other person, their issues, and their previous experiences in life. So don't take it personally."

It took a couple of years for me to fully embrace this concept, but I am glad I did. Sometimes you have to separate the person from the behavior. On many occasions it saved me the aggravation of hurt feelings, resentment, and anger. Not taking things personally has also empowered me to forgive those whose actions were inexcusable. It isn't that I excuse the bad behavior of others, but I recognize that hurting people hurt people as well. So I choose to empathize. I see through the person's rudeness or insensitivity and acknowledge that it may be their circumstances and history that have resulted in them behaving the way they do. It doesn't excuse the behavior, but it does explain it. And it can keep you from allowing people to push your buttons and get an automatic reaction from you based on their negativity.

This week, I invite you to choose empathy in place of a negative reaction to a difficult person in your life. Rise above the situation. Rather than allowing their negative behavior to push your buttons, choose to respond peacefully.

Emotional baggage can cause a person to mistrust, mistreat, and misuse people in the present because of the deeds done to them in their past. So they may be talking to you, but from an emotional perspective, they are reliving old conversations that may not have anything to do with you. Refuse to allow a joyless person to steal your joy. Whether the difficult person is a family member, coworker, friend, or a stranger, don't take it personally.

To be clear, I am not suggesting that you do not stand up for yourself or speak the truth in a spirit of love. I am suggesting, however, that you do not try to figure out what you did wrong or blame yourself for "causing" the behavior of others. You are not responsible for anyone else's behavior, and when you assume responsibility for someone else's behavior, you become a part of the problem. When you encounter difficult people, here are two ways not to take things personally:

Respond Rather Than React

A reaction is automatic. A response is thoughtful. It requires you to step back for a moment, take a deep breath, and gain the perspective you need to answer a situation maturely. Often this results in changed behavior in the future. Some people are only looking for your reaction, and when you stop giving them the reaction they want, they lose control of you and lose interest. Often they move on to bother someone else who will give them the reaction they are looking for.

Set Clear Boundaries

Choosing empathy is not synonymous with being a doormat for people to step on or disrespect just because they have issues that have yet to be resolved. When a conversation needs to be had, don't hesitate to have it. When swift action needs to be taken to protect yourself from the negative actions of others, take it.

What are you taking personally right now? How could you respond rather than react to them? What other people do and say—whether negative or positive—is a reflection of where they are emotionally and spiritually. Let your response to the negative behavior of others reflect who *you* are: an emotionally and spiritually mature individual who chooses to rise above strife to be a beacon of love, truth, and respect.

Keeping Up with the Joneses Will Keep You Eternally Busy

Do you sometimes compare yourself, your accomplishments, or your possessions to others? It can be tempting and often destructive to efforts to lead a productive, self-care lifestyle. When you make constant comparisons, it can motivate you to pursue some goals and activities for reasons that are not authentic to you. Our culture seems obsessed with comparisons—from lists of the richest, sexiest, and most beautiful people to whole television shows dedicated to describing how much more fabulous someone else's life is than yours. It can be an uphill battle to be fully content with who you are and where you are in life. It's easy to believe that the grass is greener on the other side, but it never is. We all have a different history, a different set of circumstances, different advantages and disadvantages in life. Resist the temptation to compare and you will eliminate a major source of wasted time. Here are some of the most common ways people make comparisons. Do any of these resonate with you?

- *Outward appearance (clothes, hair, looks)*
- *Possessions (house, car, bank account)*
- *Children (Are yours doing better than someone else's, for example?)*
- *Achievements*
- *Job titles*
- *Performance (on the job, academics, physical fitness, etc.)*
- .... *(You fill in the blank.)*

In a world that constantly gives us images of success that prize looks, money, and fame, it can be easy to fall into a habit of trying to live up to unrealistic expectations. It's like being in a race and constantly looking around you to see who is gaining speed and who is falling behind. One of the most important keys to happiness is to stop comparing yourself to others, and be sure to identify your own measure of success.

MY CHALLENGE TO YOU TODAY
Consider the choices you have in handling a situation that is currently frustrating you. Make a choice that will lead you to greater peace, joy, and serenity in a relationship or situation in your life.

FIVE-MINUTE JOURNAL
What lesson is being offered to me through the frustration or discomfort I am experiencing in a particular area of my life right now?

One-Minute Meditation

Grant me the serenity to accept the things I cannot change,
courage to change the things I can,
and wisdom to know the difference.

"THE SERENITY PRAYER"

DAY 28

Don't Miss
the Journey

> I used to have so much to do for everyone else that
> I simply didn't "have time" to do the things that are
> important to *me*. My life had become all about
> what's important to everyone else. I've changed
> that. I'm learning to take care of myself and enjoy
> the journey. It's funny . . . everyone else in my life
> seems happier to be around me now.
>
> —LISA, 32

I just opened the blinds on the bay windows in my sitting room
this morning. To my delight, purple-and-orange-hued clouds are
gliding quickly by in the distance as the sun slowly makes itself
known. I cannot see the sun. It is still dawn. But I know that
daylight is coming and the stillness of the early morning will
soon give way to bustling life. It is moments like these that compel me to slow down and notice the beauty of the world around
me. If I never took a minute intentionally to sit still, I would
rarely experience moments like these. The sunrise occurs in the
quiet backdrop of our lives and never waits for us to notice it. It
is like much of life's precious moments—they can come and go

without our noticing, but once gone, we often long for them to return.

In the few minutes since I started the last paragraph, the clouds are no longer purple and orange—just a soft blue. That quickly, the majestic hues are gone. I'm so glad this morning that I opened the blinds when I did.

What blinds do you need to open in your life right now? Is it a relationship inviting your attention or perhaps a child growing up before your eyes? Maybe it is the need to acknowledge your progress in a particular area of your life or celebrate a milestone. Perhaps your paycheck comes and goes, and you haven't noticed that you aren't saving enough to eventually retire and stop working. Whatever the case, today I invite you to be intentional about taking simple moments to acknowledge the beauty of life as it happens.

More than your activities becoming squeezed out, busyness numbs you to the joys of everyday life. It's like you become de-sensitized to enjoying experiences in the moment because you are not really present at any given time. Moving endlessly from one activity to the next, there is little room to celebrate the milestones or enjoy each moment. There is an incessant focus on finishing one thing so that you can get to the next. In the process of rushing through life with an overload of activities, you only skim the surface of life's experiences. This is one of the tragedies of a busy lifestyle.

When I finally realized and accepted that I was too busy, I thought that the most important benefits of revamping my schedule would be the extra rest I would get and the break from feeling constantly rushed. Those benefits were great. But I gained something else that was even more beneficial. It was the grounded feeling of fully living. Adjusting my schedule created the opportunity to enjoy the aspects of life that I had previously treated as "optional." Optional activities are the things that would add joy and richness to your life if you had the time to do them. But since so many other things vie for your time, your optional activities get cut from your schedule.

My "optional" activities emerged naturally as I reprioritized my time. Within a few weeks I was cooking new dishes from cookbooks I'd bought years earlier but very rarely used. I had a new focus on perfecting my home environment to nurture and nourish me. I created handmade pillows of beautiful fabrics I had fun selecting from design stores. Never mind that my only sewing lessons were in eighth-grade home economics class, it wasn't about *being* good as much as it was about *feeling* good. Two of my top values are creativity and beauty, so creating something beautiful brought me joy.

The most important "optional" activity was entertaining. I now had the time and space to have friends over on a Sunday afternoon for cake and conversation—without planning two months in advance. When I slowed down, I discovered a side of my personality that I had only explored in spurts—a domestic side that is just as important to me as my professional life. Perhaps for you it isn't a domestic side. But there probably is an aspect of you that is diminished by the burden of your schedule. What aspect of your life is neglected because you feel too busy?

....

....

....

Busyness steals the opportunity to enjoy the journey of life. When your life is overloaded, the quantity of what you do eclipses the quality of each experience. Every day simply becomes a race to the next item on your to-do list. It is exhausting, isn't it?

In the process of focusing forward so that you can stay in the race, you are never able to look around and notice the richness of opportunity around you to upgrade your quality of life.

When I was a teenager growing up in Colorado, I would drive westbound to go to school each day. Traveling west meant that the magnificent Rocky Mountains were immediately in front of me as I drove. Even at that young age, I would intentionally savor the view in front of me during my seven-minute commute. What a shame it would be, I thought, to take such beauty for granted. And what a shame it is for us to take for granted the opportunities around us each day to connect more deeply in our relationships, enjoy the environment around us, and notice the journey we are on.

Signs that you're missing out on the journey:

- *You have hobbies or interests you have not taken time to enjoy in over two months.*

- *You do not know what you are passionate about and haven't had time to find out.*

- *You are easily distracted from your work by things that interest you but are a lower priority on your schedule.*

- *You do not have time to attend sporting events, recitals, or other events that are important to your children, grandchildren, or a child who is a special priority in your life.*

- *You rarely have time to stay in touch with friends or family members.*

- *You don't have time to date or nurture a romantic relationship (if you are single).*

- *You don't have time to go on dates or get away for the weekend with your spouse (if you are married).*

- *There's no room in your schedule to try something new, explore a potential interest, or learn a new hobby.*

I invite you to consider the most joyful aspects of your life that you have deemed "optional" and make them "essential." And if you don't know what brings you joy, it's time to find out. Why would you want these things to be essential? Because the busier you are, the more important it is to make sure that your life is balanced in a way that nourishes your whole being. If it isn't, you will find yourself being focused too heavily on one area while neglecting other aspects of who you are. When you lay a joyful foundation on which to build your schedule, success will find you.

When my life was completely focused on work, my thoughts and conversation primarily centered on work. How boring! It is great to love what you do, but when work takes over your personal life, it creates a one-dimensional existence. You might love cream cheese icing on your cake, but if you just ate the icing without the cake—it would probably be too sweet and make you sick. The same principle holds when creating balance in your life. One of my mentors used to remind me often, "Val, if you work hard, you've got to play hard." You are more than one aspect of your life—and your journey will be much richer when your activities are multifaceted. Make joy the center of your life—and you will know what to do next.

What Brings You Joy?

When joy becomes a priority, then joyful activities must be present in your life on a consistent basis. If you wait until you have time for them, you will rarely have time. If instead you make them an essential part of your schedule, then everything else must fit around them. As we've discussed, this approach means making a mental shift from "work comes first" to "my life comes first." It ensures that the important stuff—the things that upgrade your quality of life and add richness to your experience—becomes your priority. Work then fuels your life. It becomes the thing that you get to do because it gives you the resources to live more fully and expand your options. Your aim should be to work to live, not to live to work.

A Foundation of Nonnegotiable Activities

When you make the shift and adopt this approach to working and living, you will become more productive in both. When you dedicate so much time to one activity that you neglect another area that is significant, the neglected area begins to tug at you—sometimes figuratively, sometimes literally. It's like talking on the phone when you are caring for a child. The child might be oblivious to the conversation for a short while, but eventually the child will make it clear that she wants some attention. At first it might be a simple tug at your shirt, but if you don't redirect your attention, the tug becomes a demand, cry, or a yell. My friend Priscilla described it well to me one day as she explained her changed perspective after giving birth to two boys in three years. "When I chose to have children, I made a choice to shift my priorities. Before, my life fit around my work. Now my work has to fit around my children. I owe it to them to make them a priority." It was an adjustment, but more important, it was a decision. The same holds true for your overall schedule. You must make a decision about which aspects of your life bring richness, wholeness, and healthfulness. Then build your schedule around these nonnegotiable activities. Exercise, then, is no longer optional, but a foundational component of your everyday life. Quiet time, too, becomes a part of that foundation. And regular breaks throughout the day and throughout the year are standard for you.

As we draw to a close on this 28-day journey, remember these seven keys to making your lifestyle shift permanently:

1. Your life can be different.
As simple as it sounds, this is an important concept to grasp. *Your life can be different.* When you fully internalize that statement, you tap into the power you have to make choices that lead to what you truly want.

2. Busyness does not equal productivity.
When you create a foundation that incorporates activities that naturally bring you joy, health, and rest, you become more productive in the other areas. Refuse to get caught in the trap of believing that time spent exercising, resting, or playing is time taken away from more "critical" areas such as working or doing household chores. Instead, remember that time invested in your well-being creates energy that can be poured into those areas that feel more urgent.

3. Remember that self-care is sacred.
Self-care is not being selfish, as many have described it over the years—particularly in the coaching profession. They call it being selfish "in a good way." But the premise of self-care is about gratitude and stewardship. You've been given one body, one mind, and one spirit. Doesn't it make sense to treat it as you would any irreplaceable valuable? Many people take better care of their expensive cars, which can be replaced, than they do themselves.

4. Self-neglect is not pious.

In the name of "sacrificing" for others, namely their children or families, many people insist that they don't have time for themselves. Truthfully, the more responsibility you have for others, the more critical it is to make time for a steady dose of self-care. It may take some creativity to find the time, but whatever it takes, do it. Self-neglect will catch up with you—in your health, your looks, your relationships, and even the quality of your work.

5. Let go of the guilt.

Shifting from using "leftover" time for joy, health, and rest to building the foundation for everyday life on these principles requires a new mind-set. It is a mind-set that prioritizes your quality of life and may require you to say "no" to some things you have automatically agreed to in the past. For some, this brings on feelings of guilt. Let them go. You are being intentional about how you live and doing what's best for you. That is something for which you should pat yourself on the back.

6. When you truly experience life, you don't want more. You want less.

When you live on purpose, you experience a sense of contentment with your everyday life that tames the urge to constantly want more activity. Many who are discontented are searching for meaning and joy by stacking up more accomplishments and using busyness to fill a void.

7. Stop doing what doesn't work and start doing what does.

It is amazing how often we can get stuck in a rut of doing something that doesn't work—then complaining about it rather than exploring solutions. When you make the shift to making joy your foundation, you acknowledge that certain habits you've employed in the past no longer work for you. This proactive approach is a key to taking control of your time and your life.

My Challenge to You Today

Throw out your old mode of operation. Get clear about what you will no longer do without on a daily basis.

Five-Minute Journal

How do you want to *feel* on a daily basis? What nonnegotiable activities will empower you to feel that way? Identify one activity that will give your mind a break, one activity that will reenergize your body, and one activity that will warm your heart.

One-Minute Meditation

Quiet your mind. Breathe deeply. Close your eyes. Envision yourself grounded in the foundation of daily, nonnegotiable activities that will nourish your mind, body, and spirit.

A New Lifestyle

It is not an accident that you picked up *How Did I Get So Busy?* It is time for a change and I believe this 28-day journey can be a major turning point in your life. Because of the hectic pace of our culture, you will regularly face the temptation to return to old habits. Resist it, and it will become easier over time to continue your self-care lifestyle. Expect to have some bumps along the way. We all do. But don't give up when you don't do it perfectly. Learn the lessons that are offered and step back onto your self-care path again.

Throughout these pages you've gained some very practical knowledge and key steps that you can continue to implement in the days, months, and years to come. Use this book as a reference tool that you can refer to often for inspiration, ideas, and encouragement. I would love to continue to inspire and encourage you on a regular basis, so come visit me online at www.valorieburton.com, where you can subscribe to my free weekly e-newsletter and learn about upcoming teleclasses and seminars about living a more fulfilling, less stressful life.

As our journey comes to a close for now, there are three concepts I want you to be sure to remember:

1. Make a heart-to-heart connection daily.

The people in your life must be a priority. It doesn't matter how much you accomplish in life if your relationships are a mess. One of the biggest tragedies of busyness is the missed opportunity to connect with people authentically. Treat people well—even the ones you don't know. Make time for the people who matter. Love them with all your heart. And let them love you back! Remember that it isn't just about giving love, but learning to receive it as well.

2. Lasting change comes from within.

It is not what you need to do that you must remember most. It is who you become in the process of living a self-care lifestyle. You become the kind of person who has the courage to say "no" to activities and opportunities that do not serve a purpose or meet your personal priority criteria. You become the kind of person who puts family first and work second. You become the kind of person who has the integrity to align her actions with her stated priorities. Once you become the person you were meant to be, you will intuitively know what to do.

3. Don't miss out on the journey.

You deserve joy every day. And it's tough to find joy when you are overloaded with activities and rushing from one thing to the next. It's hard to find joy under those conditions because you are unable to live in the moment. Take your joy seriously. Have fun at least once a week. And celebrate your milestones. In fact, now that we are coming to a close, it looks like you have another small milestone to celebrate!

Thank you for the privilege of serving as your coach and friend on your journey toward a more fulfilling, less stressful life. I hope our paths cross again!

Warm wishes,

Valorie

acknowledgments

A special thank-you to Michael Palgon, for your vision. I am grateful for the opportunity to write this book with Broadway.

Ann Campbell, what a true joy to work with you as my editor! Thank you for your encouragement, skill, patience, and genuine enthusiasm for helping me help readers to reclaim their schedules and make self-care a priority.

Tommy Semosh, Catherine Pollock, Beth Meister, and the entire marketing and sales team at Broadway, thank you for your enthusiasm and hard work on the marketing and publicity for this book.

To my husband Charles, *the love of my life*. I so appreciate your partnership, love, and belief in me.

To my mother, Leone Murray. Thank you for being a true inspiration—and a fabulous scheduling manager!

To my father, Johnny Burton, Jr. Thank you for always sharing your love and encouragement.

To my little brother, Wade Murray. Thank you for being you and always so supportive of your sister!

Thanks, Monica Donald and Kendra McGee, for helping grow Inspire Inc. and keeping the journey fun and joyful.

To you, the reader. I love connecting with you through the written word. On our journey together through these pages, it is a privilege to be your friend, coach, and catalyst for positive change!

about the author

Valorie Burton has helped thousands of
people find the courage, clarity, and tools
to make meaningful life changes. A sought-
after speaker and professional certified
coach, she is the author of *Listen to Your
Life*, *Why Not You?*, *What's Really Holding
You Back?* and *Rich Minds, Rich Rewards*.
She has served clients in more than thirty
states and seven countries. A regular media
contributor, she has appeared in *Essence*, *In
Style*, the *Los Angeles Times* and hundreds of
television and radio shows. Valorie and her
husband live in the Washington, DC, area.
Subscribe to her free weekly e-newsletter at
www.valorieburton.com.

NOTES

NOTES

NOTES

....
....
....
....
....
....
....
....
....
....
....
....
....
....
....
....
....
....
....
....
....
....
....

NOTES

....
....
....
....
....
....
....
....
....
....
....
....
....
....
....
....
....
....
....
....
....
....
....
....

NOTES